Praise for *Seeking Parmenter*

Seeking Parmenter is a unique and lyrically written memoir that is not focused on the author's relationships with people, but rather a family's relationship with place. What becomes so evident from Butterfield's return as an octogenarian to his childhood farmscape is that both landscape and people intricately mold each other.

—**Tom Wessels**
Author of Reading the Forested Landscape *and* Forest Forensics; *Former Director of the Environmental Biology Program at Antioch New England Graduate School*

Brought vividly to life for us in this succinct memoir is a subsistence farm in southern New Hampshire that was in continuous operation from 1800 to 1960. During all of that time it was in the good hands of one family progressing through fully six generations. The author, who grew up on the farm during its final agricultural years, with access to extensive family diaries and other records, as well as to relevant town reports, has been able to offer us a fascinating play-by-play description of the evolution of farming, with all of its ups and downs, sounds and smells, and sweeping drama through the passage of those 160 years of enormous technological advances and social changes.

And thus beginning in 1960, with the farm still in the same ownership for now even two further generations, the open land is being quietly reclaimed by nature, a phenomenon of old-field forest succession that the author has been continually observing and analyzing with awe and devotion. So here we have a volume not only of importance to the many descendants of our early New England's hard-scrabble farmers, but one that will as well broaden and otherwise enrich anyone devoted to American history on the one hand and to New England's ecological dynamics on the other in its slow recovery when human disruptions cease.

—**Arthur H. Westing, M.F., Ph.D.**
Putney, Vermont, 17 April 2015

Observational, poetic and refreshingly nonjudgmental, *Seeking Parmenter* twines the human and natural history of a classic New England farm into a seamless narrative told through the author's journey across the landscape and time. We should all be so lucky as Charles Butterfield to have such a lifelong attachment to a place on the land."

—**Ryan Owens**
Executive Director, Monadnock Conservancy

Seeking Parmenter is a moving and evocative exploration of the intertwining of place and history. Charles Butterfield grew up on a rural farm in southern New Hampshire. In this "memoir of place," he returns to his childhood farm and shows us what it might mean to be open to the presences of the past that are inevitably embedded in the places where we find ourselves. And with the eye of a naturalist Butterfield sees the ways in which the many other beings who live in places change over time, including those with roots and leaves, as well as feathers and fur. Full of fascinating observations, at times lyrical, *Seeking Parmenter* is an intelligent and beautiful book. It is also a wise book, inviting us on a journey of understanding our own place in a more-than-human world.

—**William Edelglass**
Professor of Philosophy and Environmental Studies, Marlboro College
Coeditor of the journal, Environmental Philosophy

SEEKING PARMENTER

a memoir of place

*For Phil
With love,
Charlie*

Charles Butterfield

Pen and Ink Drawings by Chuck McLean

HOBBLEBUSH BOOKS
Brookline, New Hampshire

Copyright © 2015 by Charles Butterfield

All rights reserved. No part of this work may be used or reproduced in any manner whatsoever without written permission from the publisher, except in the case of brief quotations embodied in critical articles and reviews.

Composed in 11.1/14.3 Monotype Bembo Book with Neue Haas Unica Pro display at Hobblebush Books

Printed in the United States of America

Pen and ink drawings and map by Chuck McLean

ISBN: 978-1939449-10-8

Library of Congress Control Number: 2015945875

HOBBLEBUSH BOOKS
17-A Old Milford Road
Brookline, New Hampshire 03033
www.hobblebush.com

Contents

MAP   2
PREFACE   3

Part I
Seeking Parmenter   9

Part II
Walking a Wall   25

Part III
Where Parmenter Flows   63

Part IV
Parmenter Without Us   117

GEORGE PARMENTER'S OBLIGATION   135
THE GENERATIONS   139
NOTES   143
ACKNOWLEDGMENTS   147

ALSO BY CHARLES BUTTERFIELD

Poetry
Another Light (with Larry Richardson)
Field Notes

Biography
In the Shadow of Cedars

to Nancy

*Scratch a name in a landscape
and history bubbles up like a spring*

CHET RAYMO

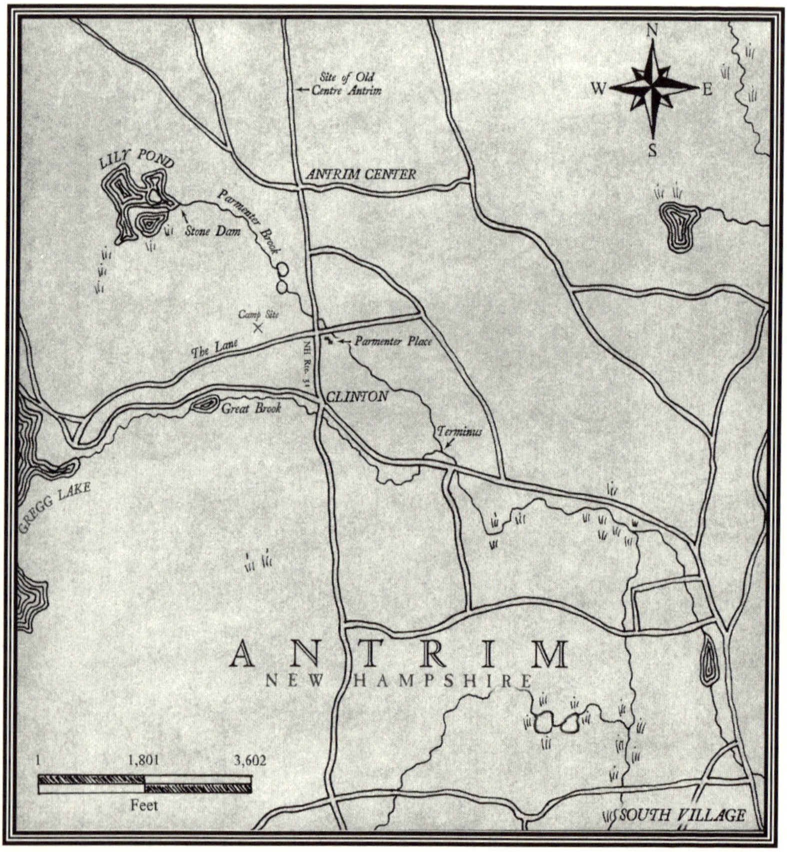
N
W
E
S
Site of Old Centre Antrim
ANTRIM CENTER
LILY POND
Parmenter Brook
Stone Dam
Camp Site
The Lane
Parmenter Place
NH Rte. 31
CLINTON
Great Brook
Terminus
GREGG LAKE
ANTRIM
NEW HAMPSHIRE
1
1,801
3,602
Feet
SOUTH VILLAGE

Preface

Walking the rural highway (NH Route 31) between Antrim Center and Clinton Village, I reach the old Parmenter farm. My eye goes to the large sign propped up in a field grown wild:

FOR SALE—33 ACRES

But when I look across the ragged open space and into the disheveled woods beyond, I see something else.

I picture Guernseys feeding. Across a stone wall men build a load of hay, the hayrack drawn by a single large horse. A chubby woman emerges from a henhouse carrying eggs in a pail. Her daughter opens the shutters on a slab-sheathed roadside stand. Behind the stand, a ten-year-old boy moves on his knees down a long row of beans, sliding a bushel basket beside him as he picks.

I can also imagine a bulldozer scraping wide swaths of the second-growth field's dark soil, heaps of sand and gravel to one side. Concrete forms are stacked beside the stone wall. The old pasture is being shaped for something, but I can't tell what. A house with two-car garage? A gardening center? A mini-mart? An animal shelter? There is no point in letting my imagination range at will. Time will tell, for there is no idle land.

I pass by the neglected field and meet a slim, young woman, mother of Amos Parmenter's great-great-great-great-great-grandsons, tugging out poison ivy roots and sumac shoots to prepare places for her perennials beside a stone wall Amos laid up along the road well over 200 years ago. She shows me some of the pieces of equipment she has unearthed in her digging—part of a peculiarly broad-tined dung fork (we guess), a section of scythe blade, half a heavy gate hinge, the hub of a wooden-spoked cart wheel. She has placed the relics on top of the wall to set off her bright day lilies.

2

When I was a senior at the University of New Hampshire, in 1953 and '54, the faculty introduced an elective course called Senior Synthesis. I elected to enroll in this survey of academic fields, and for a dozen evenings (as I recall) I heard spokespeople for several departments describe the nature of their disciplines. Some of these areas I was familiar with, majoring in biology, but many others—engineering, philosophy, anthropology, art, economics—I knew little about.

To tie their lectures together, the professors traced the historical development of their chosen fields. The reiterated message that new ideas build on old had a great deal to do with how my world view developed. I am not afraid of change. I expect it. In many instances I welcome it.

I embrace *emergence*. Out of present conditions something different will come. "Something-more from nothing-but," is a principle of evolution. It means that any new modification arises from parts already present. It is what comparative anatomy teaches us. I see that principle at work everywhere. I believe it is a law of nature. What emerges is not necessarily more comfortable or more beautiful than the parent conditions, and in many quarters humans play a crucial role in guiding emergence (alas, often with unintended consequences), but we make ourselves grumpy and cynical as we grow increasingly alienated if we fail to recognize that something-more is emerging from nothing-but everywhere and all the time.

3

What is emerging on the old Parmenter place, and from what is it emerging?

The name Parmenter appears frequently in the earliest records of Antrim, New Hampshire. But as I use it, and think about it, it is more than a surname, ancient as its derivation from 16th century Huguenot *Parementier* (*fitting* or *finishing* as by a tailor or seamstress) may be. My Antrim ancestors did not choose their name, nor could the first to arrive foresee that within a couple of generations the name would disappear from town rolls altogether. Yet Parmenter persists. Amos's genes are expressed today in some of Antrim's people.

The name endures in Parmenter Brook, the stream that originates in the town's earliest settlement and flows around what was once the industrial hub of Antrim. Too small to power that industry, the eponymous brook was an essential resource to farmers. And Parmenter persists in the name I give to this land along the brook that Amos cleared of forest and that sustained generations of his descendants, whatever their names.

Parmenter, to my mind, represents an early American

idea—that one can leave familiar and stable territory and strike out for the unknown and through dint of labor and with faith and a little luck shape one's life and environment.

This is how thirty-year-old Amos Parmenter's search for a new home is told:

> *He had great difficulty in finding the town, then called in common talk 'Enterum,' a pronunciation not yet dead. He traveled several miles northwest of Antrim, was displeased with the land, and was on his return home* [to Framingham, Massachusetts]; *but, on being told again of this township, he turned back and bought twenty-five acres on which there was then a small house, which seems to have been built and occupied some years by Taylor Joslin. The rest of his large farm he bought and cleared.*

Parmenter has yet another, personal, meaning.

When I was six or seven years old, my grandmother took me for a long walk from our farm to a cemetery created in the 1820s close by the site of the Central Society Meetinghouse that Amos Parmenter founded and where he served as deacon for forty years. We ate our picnic under a butternut tree near Deacon Parmenter's headstone. Afterwards we strolled among the graves of his immediate family, reading the encrusted tombstones, working out relationships. This adventure, I understood, was my initiation into my clan.

4

Seeking Parmenter is not a family history *per se*, or a treatise on old-field succession. Rather, it is an informal search for a family and the environment in which they lived and worked and had their influence on their contemporaries and, in the long run, me.

For consecutive summers since 2008, I have camped alone on Parmenter land I farmed seven decades ago and later inherited and passed along. Though I moved away from the family farm to follow a career in education, my long life grew from here. I derive my love of the land from what I experienced here as boy and young man. This memoir is my attempt to act on a tenet of my faith which writer Anne Michaels puts this way: "If you can learn to love one place, sometimes you can also learn to love another." In my case, that other place is emerging from what was. Right here.

I

Seeking Parmenter

There is only one single urgent task:
to attach oneself someplace in nature.

RAINER MARIA RILKE

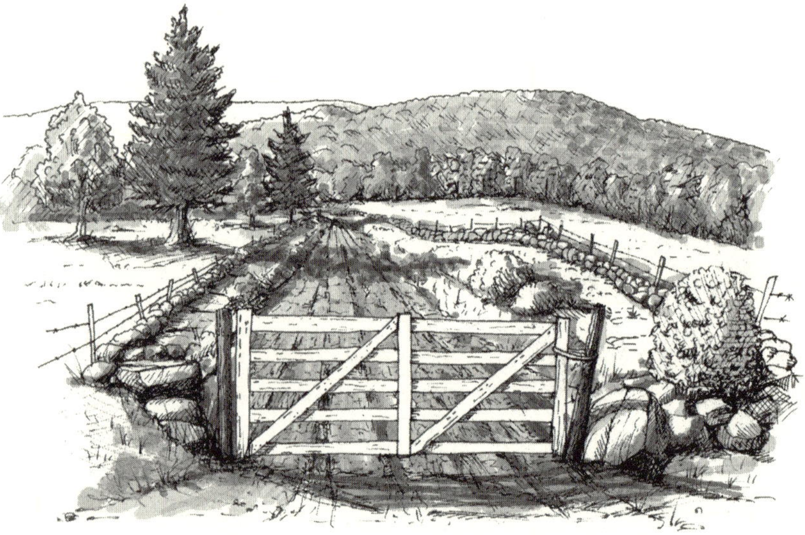

Through the underbrush and ferns to my left and right, I see the granite ghosts ox-drawn and levered into place to mark the right-of-way of one of the oldest roads laid out in the small town of Antrim in south-central New Hampshire. On this overgrown trail, scarred once with deep wheel ruts, I stumble past the site of the old Parmenter cabin. Where I go, alone and loaded with camping gear, the Parmenter children watched sleds pass by bearing logs to Samuel Gregg's sawmill and carts carrying grain to be ground.

Now labeled "private way" on Antrim's tax map, this wide path, cleared of tree stumps in the 1790s, was a major business route through the town's center for eighty years. After the town voted to "give up" the road in 1873, it was incorporated into the Parmenter farm which had grown up on both sides, and for 100 years "the lane" continued to serve my family, linking cow pasture to barn, woodlot to woodshed, and providing a shaded shortcut from itchy haymow to cool Gregg Lake. I am lugging my tent and sleeping bag up the same wet hill my great-great-great-grandfather's oxen trod pulling firewood and produce, mired, as they must have been at times, where underground springs still flow and soak my boots. My campsite, on land Amos Parmenter cleared early in Thomas Jefferson's presidency and which I owned (at a distance) for thirty-five years, is partway up this soggy slope.

Just over the wall, south, stands a set of new buildings amid well-kept gardens and extensive lawns that reach far into what I recall as hemlock forest. This *House and Garden* setting was a piece of Amos Parmenter's farm that my sister and I gave to her youngest son. Graded and smoothly mowed, the land bears no signs now of Parmenter's usage or of my father's side-hill pasture that hosted a single pear tree.

One day, my boyhood companion and I decided to use the pear tree in the manner of a rodeo chute to mount the back of one of my father's milk cows. Ben caught and led the heifer under the tree. I slipped from a low branch onto the cow's spine to be exploded into the rocky pasture. My father, learning of our misadventure, used the occasion to reason with us not about the stupidity of our risking skull and limbs, but of traumatizing his cow and negatively affecting her milk production.

On this land five generations of farmers' sons learned to think first about the welfare of productive livestock. I have come here, in part, to find whatever traces remain of fathers and sons figuring out together how to make this hard earth yield.

2

Terry Tempest Williams describes a writing exercise she calls *repetitions*. It begins with her writing a sentence, the topic being whatever she is trying to get her mind around at the moment. Then she writes another, different sentence directly on top of the first. That is followed by a third, a fourth, and so on. A whole paragraph can pile up as a single, undecipherable line on a scrap of paper. The process, she finds, leads to a clarification of her thinking and to the thing she really needs to say. "As my black pen circles back on itself, destroying as it creates, hiding what has just been written as another sentence walks across the newly exposed words, I am freed."

To find what I want to say about this place, I am putting my words over the sentences already written into this land. The difference between Williams's exercise and mine is that to clarify my thinking I look for clues in the underlying sentences. Through the ferns and under the trees, I seek fragments of what others laid down prior to my excursions.

I hike between stone walls set two rods apart, the standard width of town roads once. Though the walls are deep in cluttered woods, here and there I see gaps, intentional openings built into the walls to accommodate carts or herds leaving and entering the road. From the pattern of trees growing, and signs on the ground visible through these gaps, I read the land written over by forest.

"In the process of layered language a path is cleared." For Williams, sequentially obliterated lines culminate in a thought. For me, the layered evidence of land use culminates in the *now* of this land. I am walking through all that that past has come to be, not a culmination for all time, but for today.

"Who we are now is all that has happened before us, happening as us, in the now." Paul Rezendes goes on, "All our ancestors and everything they did, every decision they made, everything they learned is happening now. And our ancestors are not only people—but also the river, mountain, rock, fire, land, ocean, forest, bobcat, and deer."

Where I walk is chiefly hemlock-beech-oak-pine forest, typical second growth (actually third, fourth and more growth) in south-central New Hampshire. These trees have claimed their inheritance from the farm that was, before them, wrenched, pasture and field, from the generations of prior woods and habitats that stretch all the way back to the bare boulders and gravel that emerged from under the last glacier. This land is layered language.

And in the topmost layer the deepest sentences of my life were written. Though for twenty years farming was in my muscles, it was not in my blood. Music and literature and science lured me to the state university and from there to places where I made a long career of high school science teaching, with music and poetry on the side. Now, written atop all that has gone before, comes an imperative: Go back to the place where your story began and see what you can make of it.

3

I hear low rumbling from the west. It is mid-afternoon. Hot, muggy. I have stripped to bare essentials. The mosquitoes and deerflies have been waiting in these woods for their first meal of manblood, and they are glad to find the exposed parts of me. Gary Snyder's observation comes to mind: "The usefulness of hair on legs: mosquitoes and deerflies have to agitate it in drawing nigh the skin—by that time warned—Death to Bugs." But I am weighed down with a backpack, and I carry my stuff-sacked tent in one hand and a rolled-up air mattress in the other. My sleeping bag is tucked under one arm. Insects are at liberty to feed on me until I can swat them at the campsite a couple hundred yards ahead. While the skies complain, seventeen attackers meet their *zizzing* doom on the sticky deerfly patch fastened to my cap.

This is the last of four trips I will make this afternoon. On this bug-infested, abandoned cow path I have carried clothes, food, books, a lawn chair and folded cot. I have hauled enough stuff from the edge of the highway to allow me ten comfortable days and nights alone on the old Parmenter place.

One thing I don't have to lug is water. Not a hundred feet from my tent site is the rock-walled natural spring that supplied water for a century and a half to people, chickens, cows, sheep, hogs and horses on our farm. I have only to slide its heavy wooden cover to one side and dip up a bucket of clean, cold spring water whenever I need it. This good water is all mine. People and animals at the farmstead where I grew up depend these days on a deep well drilled in the dooryard.

Thunderheads are massing. At the gap in the stone wall enclosing a former orchard, I drop my gear, unpack the folding shovel and grub out a shallow trench, outlining the four edges of the eight-by-eight-foot tent floor. I hope my shallow ditch collects and wicks away the rain so that it doesn't pool under the ground cloth. Roots and rocks slow my progress. On the bright side, fore-storm wind is picking up, flushing the blood-sucking *Chrysops* from the area. I smooth the ground cloth within the dimensions of my moat, and scramble to unfurl the tent and its fly.

My L.L.Bean tent is beautifully designed to shelter me from a thunderstorm. Its screened windows and doors, each with an awning, and its multiple storage pockets sewn into the walls, provide all the comfort and convenience I need. Suspended as it is from flexible, curved poles that crisscross to form an exoskeleton, I sacrifice no space inside to tent poles. As long as I execute the steps in correct sequence I can have the tent up in less than ten minutes. I figure there is just about that much time to batten down. Before I have the tent fly completely secured, heavy drops fall singly through the pine and hemlock branches overhead. Fly tied down, I toss my gear inside, climb in myself, and zip the door. The skies burst.

I can imagine I'm trapped inside a snare drum. Cannons are firing directly over my head. Winds fierce as battle smoke swirl around the tent. Dry, and presumably safe inside plastic threads, I unroll the air mattress, spread it out on the cot, and lie down to recuperate. Despite the warfare outside, I fall asleep.

Silence wakens me. The storm was brief and has moved on. Sunlight slips through breaks in the overhead foliage, illuminating the woods around me like a stage set. A light breeze shakes water drops on the tent in a random, arrhythmic tattoo.

4

While I wait for leaves to dry off, I flip through notes in my journal. To tell the story I want to tell, I needed to have key points of Antrim's past and its geography straight in my mind. I can't carry my tender volumes of town history into the damp woods, so I have front-loaded my journal with notes. Not far from where I sit in the woods there were at one time Amos Parmenter's brick meetinghouse with ornate belfry and tiered steeple, a schoolhouse, twenty houses, six mills, a store, a blacksmith shop and a cooper's. Except for the houses, everything else is gone.

I wanted to make sure I had pinned down the history of my family before I tramped over the land they lived and died on. Amos himself was descended from enclosed-farm, East Anglian

Puritan stock. His ancestors were among those who founded the town of Sudbury, Massachusetts, in the 1630s. Through his wife, my great-great-great-grandmother Tryphena (née Bannister), who bore eleven of her dozen Parmenter children in a cabin less than a hundred yards from my tent site, I can trace my lineage to Francis Cooke, wool comber, who arrived on the *Mayflower*.

My journal was bulging with notes long before I brought it under these trees, and it contains this passage penned just before I left home for my sixth consecutive summer—different years, different months—of camping at the place where my ancestors settled.

Why do I make these serial returns to a place where the land use is not as I knew it? Why come back to where there are only shades of people I knew and loved or knew about? Why does an old man revisit the place where a young man's thinking focused on his long future? The answers I liken to a mountain experience.

When I climb Mount Monadnock there are spots on any trail I take where, just below the summit, I can rest while I survey the long way I have come. Studying my accomplishment gives me the push I need to mount the top. Now in my ninth decade, there is not likely a long climb to my own summit, and looking back there is a deep view.

Back to inheriting this family farm with my sister and passing pieces of it on to her children and grandchildren.

Back to my boyhood joy of raising animals and enduring the concomitant drudgery of farm chores while boys not much older than I went off to World War II.

Back to my father, hanging up his gas mask from World War

I and exchanging his artillery-officer uniform for overalls to work this, his father's poultry farm, out of debt.

Back to my grandfather acquiring the farm from his father, along with guardianship of his younger siblings, when my great-grandmother committed suicide, and her poultryman husband, though he defended Lincoln's capital against the Confederates, could not cope with such a loss.

Back to my seventh-son-faith-healer-jack-of-all-trades-great–great-grandfather buying this place from his father under crushing obligations intended to guarantee the older generation the convenience and safety they felt entitled to.

Back to his father, raised in America's first generation, clearing this land and fathering this town, and who, as Antrim's representative to the State's General Court, feted General Lafayette's triumphal return to New Hampshire in 1825.

"Who we are now is all that has happened before us, happening as us, in the now."

And it is the now I'm here to see. What I want to know is how has Parmenter's land fared since he worked it? Can I still find the outlines of his pastures, hay fields and woodlots? What has grown over my grandfather's chicken ranges and my father's cow pastures? Do red spruce still grow where generations of Parmenter and Butterfield boys cut Christmas trees? Walking home from school in October I invariably swung through the orchard behind the barn to snatch a McIntosh or two for fortification before starting chores. Do those trees yet bear fruit?

5

To study this forest-to-farm-to-forest landscape, I have selected two transects to guide me.

One of these is a stone wall just short of half a mile long that marks the original north boundary of Amos Parmenter's farm. Walking the wall from east to west, I will cover pasture, cropland and orchard, woodlot and timber stand. The wall is an artifact, and the traces of plots laid out beside it are artifacts, too. Along the wall lies the history of farming on the Parmenter place.

Of great importance to the operation of the farm and of particular interest to me as a boy, Parmenter Brook, my second transect, cuts through about a third of the remaining Parmenter place. Here I fished for brownies, lured bullfrogs with a cloth-baited hook, dredged and dammed a swimming hole that turned into an ice rink where I skated until my ankles went crazy. I will trace the brook from its Lily Pond source to its confluence with Great Brook, the industrial river that once powered the town. Parmenter Brook is my link to the political and economic context of Amos's life and the lives of his Antrim descendants.

There is a psychological dimension to these serial sojourns as well. I come here anticipating, even expecting, that I will discover why this place has such a strong hold on me. But what, in point of fact, can I learn firsthand by hiking these woods and wading this stream for ten days at a time? What are the lessons this brook and this wall can teach me at my age? I tell myself this is more than a trip down memory lane. But, I ask myself, what insight will I develop, what new appreciation of this environment will I gain as I experience the grown-over farm close up?

I cannot deny my sense of loss when I walk over what used

to be our farm. Ecopsychologists call my emotion *solastalgia*. With its echo of nostalgia, and roots in Latin *solacium* (comfort) and Greek *algia* (pain), solastalgia stands for what I feel when I acknowledge that the place I love is under immediate assault, a form of homesickness while I'm at home. In that mood, I regard sumac shrubs crowding McIntosh apple trees I once harvested as environmental degradation.

But solastalgia is fleeting for me. What captures my imagination is the endurance of things. One October afternoon I walk among those McIntosh trees behind the barn and pick apples just as I did seventy years ago. The steadfast trees, for many intervening years dropping their wasted fruit among wild blackberry canes and sumac bushes, this day yield apples to me as if they have been waiting for me a long time and welcome my return. For a few lovely minutes, nothing has changed. The trees and I are free of old age. Redemption is not too strong a word for what I feel today.

Though my solastalgia is real, it doesn't last, because I am in the grip of a countering emotion called *soliphilia*.

Soliphilia is love of place. Not love of place as it once was, but place as it *is*. Left alone, any piece of land once the domain of industrious farmers undergoes change because farming abhors wildness. Industriousness relaxed, sumacs in the apple orchard signify ecological succession. Sure, it would be great fun to have the money and time to bring back the pastures, repopulate them with Guernseys, and to clean up the orchard and hang up my old sign: "Apples for Sale." But it is also fun to walk over the former farm and identify the native species that are returning now that a long agricultural disturbance has passed.

I'm not a fan of sumac, however luxuriant, but I have to ask, would these wasteland bushes thrive as they do were the soil not enriched with apple compost?

And there is this. Not original with me, but I dwell on it:

> *The speculations, intuitions, and formal ideas we refer to as "mind" are a set of relationships in the interior landscape with purpose and order; some of these are obvious, many impenetrably subtle. The shape and character of these relationships in a person's thinking, I believe, are deeply influenced by where on this earth one goes, what one touches, the patterns one observes in nature—the intricate history of one's life in the land.... The interior landscape responds to the character and subtlety of an exterior landscape; the shape of the individual mind is affected by land as it is by genes.*
>
> —*Barry Lopez*

6

My tent occupies the gap in a stone wall that defines the "Old Orchard." A century and a half ago wooden rails across this gap barred sheep and cattle from the apple trees. (In October, 1860, Amos Parmenter's son George sold thirty-five bushels of apples for $1.05 and forty-four gallons of cider for $2.75.) My campsite is fairly level and relatively free of surface stones, making for smooth and easy access to the orchard. I will live in the dense shade of tall pine and hemlock trees that have grown from saplings since active farming ended here sixty-five years ago. The large stones in the wall that border what was once cultivated land will serve as my table, chairs, and low kitchen counter/bathroom vanity for ten days, although not one of them presents a flat working surface. Smaller stones for building a fire pit are hiding under a thick mat of pine needles where they were thrown when this land was first cleared.

The grass within the old orchard has given way to poison ivy which finds sun enough to flourish under thick goldenrod, barberry bushes and juniper. Scattered rock maples and white ashes stand fifteen feet tall. Few pines have invaded the space, though they are toweringly abundant outside and along the walls. One explanation for their scarcity in the open area derives from the botany of white pine.

Not every year do pine trees produce a good crop of cones. Mast years are sometimes several years apart. The tiny seeds released from the cones encase little food reserve and so must fall on nearly bare soil in good sunlight in order to germinate. Dropping atop grass already well established dooms pine seed to high and dry failure. Meanwhile, maple and ash seeds, heavy enough to fall through grass blades and carrying within them sufficient stored food to allow them to take root in the underlying soil, have a head start over the pines, and because white pines are shade intolerant, they don't get going where taller trees are already established. In the 1930s, my father converted the old orchard to cow pasture. Since grass grew well, thanks to his vigorous encouragement, pine seeds have had a difficult time taking root where the cows fed. A single industrious farmer has lasting, though maybe not everlasting, influence on his land.

7

I am surprised how quickly the air has cleared after the thunderstorm. A weather front has moved through, and I am now under a high-pressure cell. The air is clear and dry. Breezes keep insects away. Bright sun illuminates the pasture-grown-wild behind my tent and filters through the evergreen forest gracing my front entrance. Under friendly, puffy clouds I set out for that stone wall on the far edge of his north field that Amos Parmenter looked upon from his knoll-perched cabin beside the old road. With *Trees and Shrubs of New Hampshire*, *Newcomb's Wildflower Guide*, *Ferns of Northeastern and Central North America*, and my notebook and pens loaded into my field bag, I take off. Seeking Parmenter.

II
Walking a Wall

Before I built a wall I'd ask to know
What I was walling in or walling out
ROBERT FROST

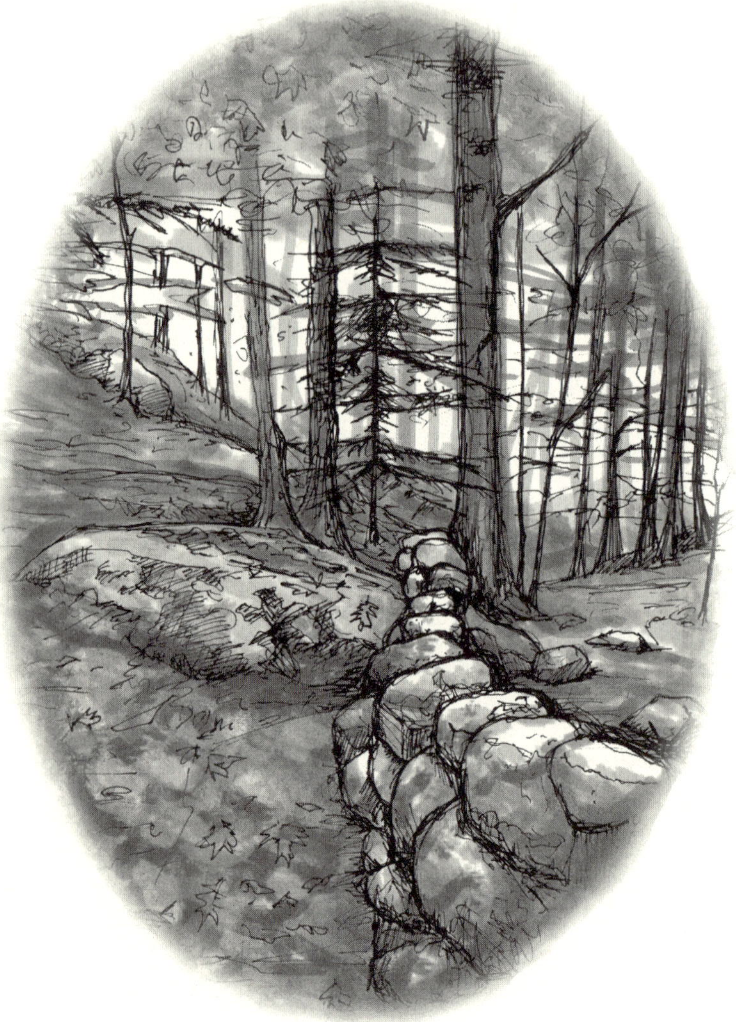

I like to imagine a mid-nineteenth century photographer positioning himself in a hilltop pasture and capturing on glass plates the walls of stone rippling over Amos Parmenter's cleared and sunny land below. The glass shows crude lines of rock separating Amos's farm from the next, his crop field from orderly rows in his orchard, his garden plots from his rock-dotted cattle pasture, and his barnyard from the right-of-way of the steep road connecting his Clinton Village to Antrim Center.

I cannot stand anywhere today to scan the limits of Amos's hard-earned acres, so lost are they in second growth, but I can walk over his farm guided by a stone wall he likely built and surely mended. From signs in the forest habitat intersected by this wall, I can interpret his workplace and that of five generations of descendant farmers, and boyhood on my great-great-great-grandfather's farm greens again like the ferns that cover rocks.

At the edge of the road in the imagined photograph (now NH Route 31), I am, according to a survey plat, at the east end of a straight boundary line of stones running through the woods ten degrees north of west about four tenths of a mile. Here where I begin it's hard to see the stones lost in the herbaceous twist and mess that has taken over Amos's farm, but ahead I see the rocks in sunlight where they climb away from my starting point in sloppy lowland.

CHARLES BUTTERFIELD

The wall I follow once separated the land owned by the first minister called to the town, Reverend John Whiton, D.D., from that of Amos Parmenter, forty-year deacon in their Presbyterian Church.

These abutters may not themselves have constructed every rod of wall. Whiton bought his land from Tobias Butler, and Parmenter acquired his place of Taylor Joslin, both deeds executed as the eighteenth century turned to the nineteenth. Butler and Joslin each arrived in Antrim, the first settlers in this part of the town, shortly after the American Revolution when our New England stone walls were just beginning to appear on the landscape, replacing fences made of brush, rails or extracted tree roots intertwined. It may have been these Scots-Irish pioneers who laid these rocks in place. Nevertheless, better known in Antrim's formative years, Reverend Whiton and Deacon Parmenter worked the land on their respective sides of the lined-up granite, meeting annually to mend their common bound.

At the edge of the highway, wall-building material is well hidden in herbaceous vegetation. Mingled spicy scent of ferns I crush as I step hangs in the air with the fungal aroma of wood duff making soil. If smells were visible, I wouldn't be able to see anything else in this fragrant habitat. I'm reminded that when my father and I were at work in the woods, he would sometimes stop what he was doing and draw in the forest smell around us. My father loved to work at anything, but he was in his element where there was the enveloping fragrance of trees.

I reach down through the aromatic three-foot-high royal, hay-scented, interrupted, and New York ferns to measure a typical wall rock at thigh height. It measures two and a half feet long, one and a half feet wide and one and a half feet thick. Calculating from the average density of granite, this volume of stone weighs in at just under half a ton, so heavy it was most likely dragged into place by a strong and steady ox. Though effort of man and beast stabilized each stone in position, the years since have worked against them, so that in places some lie scattered at my feet, pretending that their rightful place is in the weeds.

Feeling, more than seeing, stones hidden in the forest of ferns, I recall poet Wallace Stevens's lines, "...[A]n illusion so desired // that the green leaves came and covered the high rock...." I read *The Rock* as a poem about the imagination's capacity to make something lasting from "the gray particulars of a man's life." In my reading, the "illusion so desired" is to make the impermanent permanent. Here among wet fronds, I stumble over the impermanent wall, and it is my illusion, I suppose, that I can recreate something of the lives lived out around it and thus give those farmers' work a measure of permanence.

About a hundred feet west of the highway, the downfall of the wall is dramatic. Here Parmenter Brook flows from the property to the north onto my family's land. There has been time enough, the stones tell me, for the persistent flow through centuries to undermine their foundation. For a distance of some twenty feet there is no wall left standing. Every massive foundation stone has been unsettled, the grains of earth it once rested on washed downstream, causing upper stones to tilt and press against each other until all of them have rolled to the ground. Green leaves came and covered them.

I know for a fact that this destruction is not recent. No one has worked the strewn rocks back into place for at least a hundred years. This break in the wall was here seventy years ago when I stretched three strands of barbed wire across the opening as my father stapled them to fence posts. He worked with his father doing the same. All these years later, I find sagging lengths of rusted wire still fastened to fallen chestnut posts, remembering like old men the useful work they once were able to do.

Working softly, water topples boulders and carves the earth. Wherever soil would yield, the brook has etched a maze of stream beds. I cross four or five branches of Parmenter Brook within about thirty feet, the streams obscured by the dense plant life that thrives with abundant irrigation. My walking stick, doubling as third eye, sinks into the saturated land just when I need it to keep me upright as I vault from one doubtful hillock to another. Fox grape and bittersweet vines hobble my feet and lasso my shoulders. Tightly crowded elderberry bushes higher than my six feet create nearly impenetrable obstacles. Clumps of smooth alder bar me in one direction, a fallen swamp maple in another. Multiflora rose bushes with inch-long thorns grip my shirt and tear my skin. I bleed to make progress. And such a vegetable tangle I remember from decades ago.

2

When my father noticed one morning that a young cow, due to deliver any time, was missing from the herd, he sent me out to find her. She was near this fallen wall and rambling brook, her newborn, still birth-wet, crumpled in the weeds and crying out. A ten-year-old could see that this was not right. Normally, a mother cow is busy licking her calf and lowing assurances to her newborn, wobbling to its nourishment. This cow lay on her side panting, her head hard against the moist earth. Her eyes were open, but the great orbs did not shift as I came near. She made no effort to stand.

I ran back to the barn. My father, suspecting the worst, hurried to the house and phoned Doctor Tenney. Luckily for us, his new assistant was at a nearby farm and came within a few minutes. I led my father and the young vet across the pasture to the cow's dark hiding place where the new doctor made his diagnosis quickly, and immediately rummaged in his satchel for a large syringe. I watched as a calcium supplement was pushed into the cow's jugular. Within minutes, stunning me wordless, the big head rose off the ground. The cow grunted, bent her legs signaling her readiness to stand, and in no time, with our help, was on her feet, licking her upright calf, its tail whipping in anticipation.

It was not a *miracle* I witnessed here beside the wall. It was physiology. Sometimes the hormones that regulate calcium in a pregnant female, humans included, will go awry and too much of the vital mineral is drawn into milk, leaving nerves and muscles starving. *Eclampsia* can induce coma, and is fatal unless supplemental calcium is available. Administered in time, something resembling a miracle occurs in a cow pasture.

I cannot from here now see the barn, screened off as it is by the vine-shackled shrubs and trees around me. I could not possibly hurry there with catastrophic news. But once I did, and that cannot be lost in second growth.

3

I fight and bleed for every inch of advancement, but I am determined to stay close to my family's side of the wall as I continue my obstructed way west. It would be easier for me to walk on the north side where the view is decidedly more open. Over there, a few trees have blown down, and scattered sawed stumps poke up, but I can see the ground everywhere. What could explain the difference between the obscuring jungle where I am and the land nearly clear of undergrowth on the other side of this line of rocks?

Because the land north of me is open to view, I can see that the ground rises and falls in low swells. Forest landscape interpreter Tom Wessels has pointed out to me that where land is not cultivated but allowed to support trees, pillows and cradles occur over time. Imagine this: In a high wind a tall tree falls over, lifting its root pad like a ragged can lid. The depression created by the raised root mass Tom calls a cradle. Now fast-forward a few years and see in the cradle the pile of dirt that has dropped and been rain-eroded out of the decaying roots. This mound of soil and rocks is the pillow lying in the cradle, but not filling it entirely. In the meantime the tree trunk has been harvested or has rotted into soil. The irregular undulations I see across this land are cradles and pillows, the swells smoothed by accumulated forest debris.

The irregular undulations tell me that north of this wall there has been no tillage for a long time, if ever—only woodland. On this south side, while there was no tillage, I know tall trees were not allowed to grow because here there was pasture. For generations my family was feeding livestock where I stumble. On the other side of the wall firewood and timber grew.

All around me there are red maple, white ash, chestnut, and American basswood saplings vying with shrubs and ferns for the available sunlight; so in the future there may be a forest on my side of the wall because herds of domestic grazers no longer nibble their shoots. But a forest may take its time forming since the brook's periodic flooding favors herbaceous plants over woody. Anyway, while I wait for mature trees, there is good deer browse and rabbit food along the wall. As if through long-ingrained habit, my family's land still feeds the animals.

I have walked uphill onto drier terrain and out of the insect-infested wetland Parmenter Brook has created and claimed. Through the thinning ferns along the wall I can see, in places, remnants of barbed wire stapled to growing trees or leaning fence posts. I'm reminded that rock walls were not, by themselves, fences. It would be too arduous a task to lay up stones high enough to bar livestock. New Hampshire law, in Parmenter's time, declared a legal fence to be four and a half feet high. Stone walls were rarely built much taller than three feet, "thigh high." To create a fence, long before barbed wire was invented, Amos Parmenter would have topped this wall with split chestnut rails, tree roots or brush stuck into the spaces between stones, branches woven into fencing material. I am walking where beef cattle in Parmenter's day and much later my father's dairy herd fed, but it was not these naked stones alone that kept them confined.

There was a reason my father and I made fence repairs in vexing blackfly season. Not so much a reason, perhaps, as a correlation. There came a day in late April or early May when the cows were let out of the barn they had occupied all winter to run and jump in the fragrant, green grass and bright buttercups, the matrons as frolicsome as the young maids. Prior to freedom day, though, we had to check that fencing was still in place after the winter. Into the blackflies then emerging from the stream, we carried heavy coils of wire, pocketfuls of wire staples, hammers and an ax. We walked along the wall looking for places where the wire hung loose. Sometimes a strand could be looped around an existing post to tighten it. Often we had to insert a new post cut on the spot from a sturdy sapling. Where wire had broken, perhaps the result of a tree limb having fallen across it, we'd stretch new wire. All the while we cursed and, as free hands would allow, slapped the biting female blackflies and mosquitoes whining in our ears. Where I walk this buggy day, the wire is rusted, sagging, and in many places broken. No one has paid attention to the fence in over sixty years. Still, some of the chestnut fence posts stand, defying decay.

Before the blight of the early 1900s wiped the American chestnut from our woods, tall, famously durable specimens were harvested for utility poles (and many other uses). In time, these poles came down, replaced by treated lumber. The old poles were free for the taking, and my father collected all he could find. He cut them to length and split them into fence posts. These rot-resistant pieces stand where he or I worked them into the rock wall's interstices, the wood itself now a couple of centuries old.

"Shiftless," my father would say when we drove past a farm where fences were as dilapidated as this one is now. He wanted fallen rocks returned to their place in a wall, grass trimmed right up to the base, and wire stretched tight from post to post. A fence said something about the family that worked that place. A tight fence was a sign of industriousness, something my father greatly respected. To his mind, a man who couldn't keep his fences up would likely ride slipshod over his other responsibilities, too.

I walk along this wall reminded at every step of my ancestors' assiduity. That these boulder-strewn, wild acres were once productive farmland seems honorable to me. Every bushel of grain, every ton of beef, every thousand board feet of lumber harvested contributed to my family's security and to its members' self-respect. It was in working these same acres, taking pride in every well-built load of hay, that each generation's boys and girls gained their sense of family dignity. "Who we are now is all that has happened before us, happening as us, in the now."

4

Finally, I have made it through the rampant plant life, and I can see the wall's basal rocks clearly. Young trees, well spread out, create a canopy overhead. And here, where walking is easy, several hundred feet from the humming highway, a new chapter begins. The whole character of the stone wall changes. There are still big, ox-worked rocks, but there are also hundreds that are fist-sized tossed into the wall. Some parts of the wall are composed of large stones arranged in two parallel lines and hundreds and hundreds of smaller ones fill in between. In other places the loose stones simply overflow the larger. Someone has suggested that loose-stone wall construction like this presented an impediment to climbing sheep. Whatever, here the wall's composition is decidedly different from the construction I've seen elsewhere.

Where the Parmenters erected stone walls to mark a boundary, they laid out large, hefty rocks on the ground and topped them in such a fashion that upper stones usually bridged the spaces between the ones under them. Depending on the size of the available material, their walls stood as high as three or four such layered rocks. To stabilize the wall, I find that the builders inserted especially long stones, "thrufters" some called them. These traversing rocks laid in roughly at right angles to the wall's line bind and tie everything together.

Though a trained ox could draw a huge rock into place in the wall, there were situations that didn't allow sufficient room for a draft animal to work. In those cases, Amos Parmenter used his jack hook to maneuver big rocks. This oblong loop of steel, bent in such a way as to enfold the rounded cheek of a rock, had teeth at one end to grip the stone's surface; the other end of the loop caught Amos's crowbar. With his lever on a fulcrum, the jack hook lifted the rock when he pushed down on his bar. Someone shoved rollers under the raised stone. Repositioned, Amos then used his hook to pull the stone across the rollers, up an easy incline, and into position in the wall.

The Parmenters didn't have access to many flat rocks, easier to build with than rounded ones, because they're not abundant in central New Hampshire any distance away from riverbeds. Sedimentary rock, the kind that cleaves to form flat faces, is uncommon in this old part of Antrim. Like the other walls on Amos's farm, this one is built of igneous rock rounded by abrasion. So it is wobbly specimens I see, most of them shimmed in place with smaller pieces. Imagine the hazard to a man's fingers and fists as he shims a 500-pound, round-bottomed rock while an ox coupled to it by rope or a boy leaning on a levered jack hook holds it steady.

I've noticed as I drive around the Granite State that the color of stone and texture of gravel and sand exposed along roadsides varies from place to place. This strikes me as curious, but at the same time satisfying. Curious, because I imagine boulders all jumbled together within the glacial ice sheets that transported them, and so why one type of granite here and another type over there? Satisfying, because it means the rock material that I see belongs to that place in New Hampshire. The Parmenters built walls with *Clinton Village* granite, generally a dark gray color as opposed to brownish or reddish. Not a geologist's classification, I admit, but nonetheless pretty obvious to my eye.

It's evident to me as I walk over the land that the Parmenters had plenty of building material ready at hand. There are beautiful granite specimens lying all over the place that never made it into a wall. These strays, pock-roughened and coated with mats of moss and lichens, wait undisturbed where they are because the Parmenters were not going to heft any rock they didn't have to.

In the area where I walk now, sunlight streams through the canopy, complimenting the natural shading in the rock wall. An artist friend once pointed out to me that rocks in sunlit walls have four or five more-or-less distinct shadings. From a stone's skyward face, the lightest shade, rounded and irregular cheeks curve downward and faint shadows form, darkening variously with facets angling from the direct sun. In a wall, one rock reflects light onto the one next to it, or shades it, creating another variation. Beneath each rock its shadow is deepest.

Like a theme with variations, this rock wall in the sun is as inventive in shading as Bach's *Clavier-Übung*. Pianist Vladimir Feltsman says of the *Goldberg Variations*, "To me, performing the 30 variations is a process of bringing together light that is reflected in 30 different ways." This sun-dappled wall is like that.

"It is hard to know rocks," Thoreau said. "They are crude and inaccessible to our nature. We have not enough of the stony element in us."

I don't believe a man can build a good, lasting rock structure unless he has something of the stony element in him. Studying these great stones Amos worked into place in compliance with the physics of levers and vector forces and against the law of gravity, I am drawn closer to Parmenter through his feel for stone.

My father, too, had a feel for stone. A feel and an eye. Though he worked for forty years to keep a productive dairy farm under his feet, he was forced to supplement his income working as first-class carpenter and stonemason. On his knees at a formal wall, a well curbing, or a decorative pedestal, he would tell me what stone to bring to him from the pile collected for the job, a pile containing three times the number of stones he would use. From the empty space in the structure, his eye traveled to the pile and landed on the piece that would suit his need. It usually fit so well that he used only a little mortar to hold it in place, often none at all. Uncanny. I never had such an eye for spatial relations. But a stone builder needs it. So does a carpenter. It's a question whether the eye creates the artisan, or the artisanal experience develops the eye. But my father's eye helped to keep his farming enterprise afloat.

5

Return to the wall's new composition. Why am I finding this stretch, 300–400 feet, of tossed rocks right here? The answer I get comes from yet another spring chore associated with black-fly season.

Dennison Gould, an other-side-of-town acquaintance of the Parmenters, kept a farmer's journal. From 1838:

> *April 13, Began our spring work today for we are picking rocks. That's the most like it of anything I know.*
>
> *April 21, Mr. Chase and Joseph helped us today to pick rocks. That's a good job out of the way.*
>
> *April 23, Drawing rocks off our last year's potato ground. Began to plough today.*
>
> *May 2, Picked the rocks in the pasture field today.*

There were two ways for Gould to dispose of the picked rocks: Toss them into an out-of-the-way pile or add them to a stone wall. He probably did both. The Parmenters certainly did.

A rock pile on the land I'm covering this morning brings back a clear memory. Each spring my father and I, and any friend of mine who happened to be around, went into the pasture with our husky Friesian hauling a two-wheeled dump cart modified for the horse from George Parmenter's oxwork era. As Jerry pulled the heavy cart across the land we bent to pick the rocks that occupied the space where we wanted grass to grow and tossed them into the dump body. Not hard work especially, but tedious, our boredom relieved only by our taking turns driving Jerry. (Is it a youthful illusion I carry, or a fact, that my father didn't tire of any farm work he was doing?) All afternoon we loaded the cart, driving Jerry to the edge of the pasture, where with brute force we tipped up the bed and emptied it with a satisfying rumble that made the horse tremble.

We were making relatively easy work of a monotonous task. Instead of throwing rocks one by one into a stone wall, we dumped ours collectively onto an existing pile covering a cluster of glacial erratics already occupying land off to the side of the pasture. Probably the storage pile was begun by one of the Parmenters. We, as he, conserved valuable pasture space by dumping the small rocks on top of the immovable boulders.

I have come to that rock pile, actually one of two not far from the wall. Barely visible and overgrown with dewberry and poison ivy vines as they are, I might have walked past this evidence of many days' labor without noticing them. There is something about the lay of the land, I suppose, that caused me to pay attention. A detailed recollection—a day, a father, a friend, a horse—follows my recognition of the rock piles lost in the woods. Jumbled together just as they tumbled out of our cart, the rocks are a lasting fixture in the earth and an enduring part of my inner landscape. *The green leaves covered the high rock.*

Should a fieldstone mason need a supply of working material, he couldn't do much better than to raid abandoned stone piles or walls on old farms. Trouble is, they are now deep in the woods.

It was a running joke in my family that we would become rich someday when we found a market for all the rocks stored on our farm. In fact, one contractor did buy several truckloads of stone in a wall no longer serving any purpose and that happened to run conveniently close to the highway. We watched the diesel loader dump our stones into big-bodied trucks. A few hundred feet of Parmenter wall went rumbling down the road. I have looked, but my father's account book has no entry, "rocks sold." What I know is that one wall riches does not make.

Rock piles such as we made are a fairly common sight in our New Hampshire woods, but where creating a rock pile would take up valuable cultivated land, a thrifty farmer like Amos Parmenter threw his unwanted stones onto a nearby wall already taking the land out of service. Thus the wall served a dual purpose. In this case, the section of wall I'm walking marked a boundary and it also stored useless and nuisance rocks.

So then, this section of wall, filled with small rocks, is evidence of tillage. After the land was cleared of trees and the roots pulled, the soil was turned and cultivated. But which side—the Whiton side or the Parmenter, or both?

Not as obvious as the tossed-rock construction, I do notice something else about the wall, or rather the land beside it. On the Parmenter side, the earth runs higher next to the wall and slopes sharply away. The Whiton side shows no such ridge of earth. Tom Wessels, my well-bearded, forest forensic scientist-friend, points out that when land is plowed, the edge next to a wall cannot be turned, there being no room for ox, horse or tractor. Over the years, the tilled area lies a bit lower than this "plow terrace."

There are only tall trees now where I go, and that is all that I remember, but the terrace tells me that once upon a time Amos, or some descendant, regularly plowed a patch to grow a crop of some kind. As regularly as he plowed, he picked rocks, and it is these I see in the wall where I walk. The field was small, a few hundred feet on a side. I know, because that is as far as the small-rock composition extends. With everything being done by hand, including rock picking, cultivation here in New Hampshire was confined to conveniently sized patches. Within a few steps I pass along this edge of Parmenter's erstwhile grain field and come again to naked, big-rock boundary-wall construction.

Not only does the composition of the wall vary from section to section, but the quality of construction does, too. In places, the rocks are piled two on one and one on two as they should be for sturdiness and in accordance with good design. But I come, then, to large-rock sections with no evidence of such careful placement; the stones are jumbled together, stabilized in the wall by the sheer weight of each leaning on each. It is as if different workers, some building carefully and deliberately, others relying on brute strength and to hell with design, put this wall together. Maybe some parts of the wall had to go up in a hurry, as in protecting a crop from grazing livestock; other parts could be constructed more leisurely, as in marking a boundary that wasn't going anywhere soon.

Thus I hold conversation with the builders as I move along their project, and pause when I come to a huge section of ledge directly in line with the wall. Why bother with fieldstones in that case? Yet to let the ledge mark the boundary by itself would mean the wall of stones, all contiguous from beginning to end, would be incomplete and leave the property abutters unsatisfied. So they chuckled and left for me to find and smile about, two centuries after the fact, a row of small stones laid out in line over the surface of the ledge. And I do smile.

6

But why rocks, anyway? Revisit earliest New England, Plimouth Plantation for instance, and you find wood rails and pickets forming the enclosures. No rock walls. Jump ahead a couple of centuries and a hundred miles inland, to Sturbridge Village, say, which depicts the Parmenter era, and see both rail and stone fences. Gradually wood gave way to rock.

Well understood now, but only theorized in Amos Parmenter's time, it was scarifying, crushing glaciers that provided the stone for walls. Moving at their glacial pace from the northwest to the southeast, massive ice fields scoured earth to the depth of bedrock, the mass of ice so great that in places it actually depressed the earth's crust! Over many millennia the ice pressure rendered ledge into boulders, boulders into rocks, and rocks into gravel.

Eventually, after thousands of years, Earth returned to some former, warmer tilt, and the glacier's leading edges melted faster than new ice formed, and ten thousand plus years ago New England emerged from under the most recent destructive mantle of frozen water. The land lay strewn with rocks, and algae grew in the huge lakes of melted glacier.

Close to our barn there is a twenty-foot high cluster of boulders. I stand beside these giant crumbs of the earth's crust towering above my head and fantasize traveling back to the time when these glacial erratics first felt the sun's warmth. Right where I am, the ice sheet slipped ever so slowly off this pile of rubble. It would take dynamite and earth movers to rid our farm of this monument to the Ice Age. In its presence, I feel a dozen thousand years collapsing to my lifetime around this pile of rocks where my cousins and I played cowboys and Indians.

Life returned. "As the earth warmed and the continent emerged from the ice age, each of the tree species migrated but no two moved in exactly the same way," writes Elizabeth Kolbert in *Field Notes from a Catastrophe*. Over post-glacial millennia plant life took hold again, creating tundra-like conditions at first. As debris formed humus, shrubs moved in, building more humus that buried the rocks deep beneath rich soil eventually to be canopied by our now familiar trees. *Green leaves covered the high rock.*

In early America there was plenty of wood for building an immigrant's house and fencing his enclosures. As population expanded, settlers spread out and away from the coast, cutting and burning trees to clear the land where they went. Two things were happening: Fencing material was going up in smoke, and where insulating ground cover thinned with annual plowing and tilling, winter frosts penetrated. Rocks long buried beneath the soil began to move.

I think of it this way: Below ground, in winter, water in the moist soil surrounding a solid chunk of granite freezes and expands, pushing the rock up closer to the surface. Other soil particles fall into the space under the stone, preventing it from settling back. Abetting this upward thrust, moisture in the earth above the rock freezes and expands, and, incredibly, the heavy rock is actually pulled up a tiny bit to fill the void created by water expanding as it crystalizes. Pushed and pulled, the rock rises, I'm told, as much as a fifth of an inch per winter day. In time, if not this winter then next, or the next, the rock comes within reach of the plow point and hoe blade. It pokes through the ground and hampers the scythe or displaces forage grass. It must be picked up and thrown into a pile or a wall, and, discouragingly, a year or two later a new "ground potato" appears to replace it.

7

I am walking across a part of Amos's farm we still call the North Field. The designation suggests that these acres had a different function from the one I remember. This is where my father's milk cows were pastured, including that heifer with milk fever. When, if ever, there was a field of hay or grain here, I have no way to tell. But there must be some reason the designation *field* was applied and has persisted.

Amos Parmenter was a beef cattle dealer. John Nicholas sent this order from Carlisle, Massachusetts, August 24, 1826: "Mr Parmenter Sir Please to send me sum cattle if you can for beef by the barer and I will settle with you for them." On August 30, Amos recorded: "Sent to John Nicholas of Carlisle by Asa Parker ten head of cattle for beef, cost $103.50." Amos paid Asa one dollar for delivering the cattle. A month later, Amos "bought David Boyd's oxen for $52.00."

When my sister and I emptied our family home and auctioned off its contents, I kept a neatly constructed wooden, curved-top box filled with small, handwritten notes, IOU's and various legal papers dating to Amos and George Parmenter's farming days. Though many of these scraps are indecipherable

CHARLES BUTTERFIELD

and some are only fragments, they provide a picture of the Parmenters' farming. One such scrap, dated 1820, possibly Amos's inventory, lists ten horses, five oxen, five head of beef cattle and a cow. His North Field certainly played some role in his agricultural pursuits.

When Amos's son George bought the farm from his father, an excruciatingly detailed obligation was worked out and recorded along with the deed. (The obligation is given in full on page 135.) Because Amos insisted that his son give him one-half of all the farm's annual income, the agricultural activity is spelled out in the obligation. Thus, as of 1848, I know the Parmenter place produced grain, potatoes, and apples; supported a dairy herd which "shall always consist of four cows or more;" fed and housed beef cattle, pigs and chickens; and "if the oxen shall at any time do any more work than what is required in doing the oxwork of the farm, one-half the income of said labor shall go to A. Parmenter."

The North Field, the largest walled-in parcel I knew on the Parmenter place (Amos, then George, bought and sold larger tracts located away from the farmstead), probably served several functions during the ninety years the Parmenters were active. But by the time I came along, the area, watered reliably by Parmenter Brook, was pasture, not field.

For a brief interval, though, North Field had another function. Soon after George's entrepreneurial daughter Abbie acquired the farm in the 1890s, the Parmenter place became known as the Butterfield place. Abbie had eight children with her husband Bill Butterfield. Bill (never William) entered into the poultry business with his son Charles, and their enterprise thrived into the era of World War I. One of the Butterfield innovations was free-range chickens. An old photograph shows the North Field dotted with chicken coops. It makes sense to me that it was the young chickens that were given the freedom to run through the fenced-in grass. Older, egg-bearing hens and those that were dressed off for meat were housed in secure buildings conveniently located near the house and barn. (The barn itself still bears remnants of chicken wire high up in haymows, proof that even that space was pressed into service as hen quarters.)

I was, for some time, perplexed by the name *North* Field. The named area lies as much west as north of the house and barn where I lived and worked in my youth and teens. So why is it designated North Field? The answer, I surmise, comes from the fact that when Amos arrived in Antrim he settled his family in a cabin that stood, not where I grew up, but close beside the old road I now use to reach my campsite. Standing in that old road, approximately where the cabin sat, the field lies decidedly north.

Twenty years or so into his Antrim life, having acquired some wealth, Amos Parmenter built a fine, brick house several hundred feet east of the cabin in which his children were born and where his wife, Tryphena, died at age thirty-six. He and his second wife, Hannah Heald, moved into the new house in 1827. The field where I now stumble through barberry, bittersweet, juniper, a half-dozen different hardwood saplings, and where the "For Sale" sign is propped up, was oriented west of his big house, but the appellation North Field stuck, an intangible but enduring connection to my roots.

8

What tells me that I have finally walked the length of the North Field is, no surprise, a stone wall running north and south, at right angles to my east-west guiding wall. Barbed wire stretches along this wall, reminding me that we treated the North Field as a separate pasture from the one I step into next.

I could easily climb over this fence, but I choose to find the gap that was the cows' managed entry. Breaks in the walls to accommodate the passage of carts, livestock and farmers are strategically placed. Every enclosed acreage has one or more entrances. Paying attention to these openings gives an impression of the traffic pattern. For instance, the opening I find leading out of the North Field into the Old Orchard is narrow—ten or twelve feet wide only, appropriate for the passage of animals. In contrast, the entry into the Old Orchard from the old town road, the gap where my tent is pitched, is twice as wide. The wider opening allowed vehicles loaded with produce or whatever and pulled by teams of oxen or horses to pass through with plenty of room. The wider gap was the major access to the enclosed space.

Through the narrow gap and into the Old Orchard—another name incongruous with recent memory—there are skeletal remains of juniper in my way. Hard to believe, but these sprawling carcasses prove that at one time copious sunlight reached the ground that I'm treading in deep shade. It is not apple shade I'm under, though. Those trees are long gone. My father went to considerable effort, I recall, to reclaim these acres from the neglected apple trees. He pastured his cows here.

SEEKING PARMENTER

How came this Old Orchard? Both Amos and son George were forced to be entrepreneurs, though Amos exceeded George in this respect. They had to be inventive if these rocky acres were to keep their families in food, clothing and necessities. George did not keep as many animals as his father did. His daybook tells me that once he was out from under his "obligation" to his father, he earned his living chiefly by working with his oxen for the town and neighbors, and by butchering, selling hay and grain, and renting out his pastures. Did he turn one of the pastures into this orchard? Was it a go? Hard to tell. In 1862 he was selling apples at thirty-five to sixty cents a bushel, the price varying with the variety and the quality. Eben Bass, owner of Reverend John Whiton's farm in George's time, bought fifty bushels of apples from George at three cents per. These were most likely poor specimens good only for making cider.

The thing is, after the 1860s, there are no more apple transactions recorded in George's daybook. Perhaps the orchard, its name carried down three generations, was more a vision than a fact. Maybe referencing the Old Orchard so faithfully was a running joke my father never explained to me. I'm guessing.

When I worked this farm, there was a small orchard, strictly for home use, behind the barn. Located several hundred yards away from where I'm standing, a few varieties of apples still drop from the neglected trees. Though I don't recall this area being referred to as the *New* Orchard, intuition tells me that at some time in the past it was necessary to distinguish one orchard from the other. The appellation Old Orchard, like North Field, echoes another era.

9

I have climbed uphill, some parts pretty steep, since leaving the Old Orchard. The stones in the wall are consistently the larger rocks used to mark the boundary. Because the canopy, pine and maple, is thick here, there is very little browse underneath. I can see for long distances through the trees. Everywhere there are wall-size stones scattered on the ground that could have been collected and used to build wall, but they weren't. Why?

I am walking through the family woodlot and timber stand. In my days on the farm, this area provided the hardwood we burned every winter. The rocks were not in our way so they were left alone. Also, since cutting firewood or logs is a fall/winter chore, some of the time we were working in snow on top of these frost-heaved remnants of glacier action. The scattered rocks are evidence that there was no tillage here, and the absence of small rocks in the nearby wall confirms that fact.

Seventy years ago I would have found cords of wood stacked here. A cord is made of sticks four feet long, stacked four feet high in a pile eight feet long—128 cubic feet. We needed twelve of these each year to heat our large, two-tenement farmhouse.

A maple or oak tree too crooked or deformed to take for timber made excellent firewood. We would fell the tree with a two-man, cross-cut saw (before chain saws were common), then cut the bigger limbs and the trunk into four-foot lengths, splitting the larger-diameter pieces to hasten drying. We stacked the pieces on long poles laid on the ground to keep the firewood up away from the dampness, propping the pile with poles stuck in the ground at each end and braced. At the close of the cutting period, which sometimes stretched out over a couple of months, the woodlot was dotted with stacks, some holding a single cord, some multiples.

True, as Robert Frost's "The Wood-Pile" says, it happens that a stack of wood sometimes gets left in the woods to rot. Such a heap of labor left to "the slow smokeless burning of decay" is wasteful and testifies to the priority of some other farm work or to the shortage of dependable manpower.

Lyle Sturtevant—we called him Hedgehog, though not to his face—lived with his wife in a shanty he built on the edge of our woods. My father permitted Hedgehog to squat there in exchange for his cutting our firewood and helping with haying. Hedgehog was not burdened with higher ambitions. A cloud in the sky was reason enough for Hedgehog to stay home. If my father grew concerned that our wood supply was not growing noticeably from one month to the next, he'd ask Hedgehog about it. The answers varied, a little: "Been too wet." "Too cold this week, Byron." "Get to it next week." My father's indulgence explains why I, fifteen-year-old free labor, spent many winter days in this woodlot where I walk.

Ideally, wood needs to dry for ten to twelve months before it is ready to burn. Generally in early spring when snow on the ground still made for decent sledding, we carried the partially-dried wood to the dooryard where we would buck it up to stove size. When I first read Robert Frost's "Two Tramps in Mud Time" in high school it was not a literary exercise for me, but a statement of fact. One neighbor, not homeless, but living from hand to mouth, came each spring to see if we needed help cutting up our wood. My father always gave him work, and my mother gave him his dinner.

Sawing up cordwood became a form of entertainment after

another neighbor acquired a tractor with a saw rig attachment. Twelve cords of wood became a giant pile of stove-length chunks in half a day. That part was productive fun. Carrying the pieces into the two-story woodshed and stacking them solidly was not. Still, unlike some spring chores, stacking wood had an end to it. I could see my progress. It was numbing labor, though, and to pass the time I used to make up stories in which the wood changed character.

A fierce blizzard is fast approaching a destitute and isolated prairie Indian family. I must get as much food into their tepee as I can and as quickly as I can before the storm brings snow that will bury them for months. Whipped by the wind, I scurry to secure the food and fodder as the threatening clouds close in....

Something like that.

10

Tree stumps tell a story. Evidence of sawed timber, mostly hemlock and pine, are all around me here where I approach the west end of my trek across Parmenter land. I can tell the pine from the hemlock by the way the stumps have decayed. Hemlock bark is more resistant to rot than the wood it encloses, and so a ring of bark often remains after the inner core of wood has decomposed. These shells of great trees are scattered among hemlock saplings reaching for the sun. Flat-needled hemlock is efficient, photosynthetically speaking, and a little sunlight goes a long way, fueling these saplings that brighten the undergrowth even where the taller canopy shades them.

Pine, on the other hand, doesn't usually leave telltale shells of bark, nor do the young of the species thrive in shade. But like the hemlock, pinewood rots from the outside in, leaving a harder core enclosed in a punky crust. After about seventy years, a pine stump will have all but disappeared in the soil, according to my faithful *Forest Forensics* field guide. I am looking at some stumps that are well along in the decay process, but with enough wood remaining for me to guess it was maybe sixty or sixty-five years ago that these pines were cut down. If I'm right, then perhaps it was my father and I who one winter day pulled our crosscut saw through these trunks.

A crosscut saw requires two men. They kneel, facing the trunk, on opposite sides of the tree, the long saw blade between them, its teeth against the tree. One man pulls the blade to himself as the other follows the motion and then pulls the blade back. At first the blade slides easily, but as the saw cuts deeper into the tree each man feels resistance as he pulls. The men try to keep a steady pace, and it helps if both men have arms of about the same length. The trick is to find a rhythm for the back and forth motion, the give and take that cuts the wood but doesn't wear out the saw men. "Misery whip" is an apt sobriquet.

When the cut is well into the tree, a strong breeze may sway the trunk enough to pinch the blade. Or, more often, a tree will begin to lean toward the cutters and bear down on the saw due to an imbalance of limbs. A hardwood or steel wedge driven with an ax into the cut behind the saw blade usually lifts the tree enough to open the cut so that sawing can continue. Sometimes it takes several wedges to free the blade. Eventually, if all goes well, the tree will begin to tilt away from the saw, and with caution the men proceed to cut until the tree starts to fall. The blade is removed by one man while the pair retreat quickly from the base to enjoy the thunderous and satisfying crash of the great tree, its carcass much larger on the ground than the upright specimen appeared to be.

Learning to fell a tree seemed important to me when I was twelve or thirteen. I think now that it was important because crosscut sawing put me on a par with my father. We were a working team, and my contribution was as valuable as his. My father was generally appreciative of my efforts, however applied, but much of the time we had separate chores and worked apart. In the woods, though I was the novice, we shared crosscutting equally. That felt good.

What didn't feel so good was learning that I didn't know as much about tree felling as I thought. I volunteered to bring to school a thirty-inch piece of maple to serve as the pedestal for an anvil that had been given to our woodworking shop. With one of my regular companions, I went into these woods to cut down a good-sized tree. We found the perfect one, back-notched the trunk so that it would fall where we wanted it to, discussed how we would get out of the way when the big tree fell, and began to cross-cut the base. Things were going well, we thought, until as the tree tilted, it twisted and fell faster than we expected. Startled, we jumped away from the base. In our excitement we neglected to take the saw out of the cut, and as the tree twisted it pinched the blade tight between the trunk and the stump. The tree didn't fall; its high branches were hung up in another tree. We tried, but we couldn't work the saw loose. Defeated and tired we left the inclined tree where it was and went home.

On inquiring, my father learned that Ben and I had done an unwoodsman-like thing in abandoning a leaning tree in the woods. It was dangerous, he explained, because it might fall unexpectedly on a person or an animal. Late as it was in the day, he went back to the tree with us. Working with wedges long into chore time we finally took the tree down. The saw blade was damaged and never worked smoothly again. We were embarrassed by our ineptitude, and my father was exasperated. We mentioned none of this when we presented the sturdy pedestal to the woodshop teacher.

Whether we were cutting firewood or timber, my father and I took down one tree at a time, a half-dozen lumber trees cut into eight- or ten-foot logs was a day's work. It was here, also, that first Amos, then George, took down trees for lumber to sell (old receipts indicate that they were in that business off and on), but the stumps they left have long since rotted away. Evidence of the Parmenters' tree work was written over by fresh trees a long time ago. But I am connected to their work through my own and by the lay of the land around me that they knew.

Just how much land-clearing Amos did it is too late now for me to determine. He settled on twenty-five acres that had already been cleared to some extent by Tyler Joslin, invalided in the Revolution. Since Amos acquired additional land, it stands to reason that to create a farm stretching over a couple hundred acres he did clear away many trees, perhaps by "jamming."

A "jam" was created by chopping (or sawing) three-fourths of the way through the trunks of all the trees growing in close proximity. Once all the trees were readied, one tree was intentionally felled so that it pushed against the other ready-to-fall trees near it as it dropped. The whole section of forest came down at once, trees falling like dominoes, the "jam" crashing to the shuddering ground.

Dangerous? Here is an account from Antrim's *Town History*: "On this occasion the wind started the 'jam' a little too soon, and all ran for life, and Gideon Dodge, Jr., almost escaped with the rest, but was struck by a limb of the last tree that fell. Gideon, a married man, died June 12, 1815, aged twenty-six."

11

Like Amos long before us, my father and I employed animal power to twitch logs from the woods to a place for loading and carrying to the sawmill. Amos relied on oxen to move his logs, but Jerry, our strong and eager horse, did it for us. We chained together the logs we cut, two, sometimes three, at a time, and Jerry twitched them the quarter mile or more to the road where we piled them on a slight rise ready to be rolled onto a borrowed flatbed truck. They ended up at George Caughey's sawmill on Great Brook where my father worked as the sawyer.

It was fun to visit the mill on a Saturday morning and watch my father at his work. Though I was there on some errand, most likely bagging sawdust for stable bedding, I took breaks to watch my father reduce a huge log to a stack of boards. He'd roll a log onto the carriage, "dog" it in place with clamps, and then release the carriage to ease the tree trunk into the teeth of the spinning, four-foot-diameter blade to remove the slab wood. As slabs of bark fell from the log, a man or boy tossed them in a pile, free for the taking. The carriage rolled back, and my father ratcheted the shorn timber closer to the whirring teeth. At each pass he watched the blade tear into the log, screeching in protest when it encountered a knot in the wood. The sound of the sawmill spread throughout all Clinton.

As each board fell off the carriage, it was rolled away to the edging saw that squared the sides. All the while, blowers sent sawdust to the huge pile outside the mill where I was supposed to be filling grain bags with the fragrant waste.

Slab wood, like sawdust, is useful waste. It burns hot and fast in a kitchen stove or sap house arch, and in our case it sheathed the cabin my father built for a roadside stand. For three years, before World War II gasoline rationing curbed tourism, The Log Cabin supplied neighbors and tourists summering at Gregg Lake with fresh vegetables, milk, eggs, my mother's pastries, and most popular of all, homemade ice cream. The ice cream business proved so popular that my father added a slab-sided, screened-in porch and provided tables and chairs for customers.

My highly popular and very attractive sister, then a student at the New England Conservatory of Music in Boston, served as waitress during her summer vacations and attracted young males like ice cream draws flies. I, on the other hand, nearly a decade younger than she, spent my mornings digging potatoes or picking peas, beans, and corn to sell at the farm stand. But it wasn't all bad. I treated myself to ice-cream-Coca-Cola floats after work. That's how useful slab wood is.

Slabs from the mill went into my own cabin. My father taught me house construction step by step, using salvage lumber from the mill. I learned to level sills, lay in floor joists, toenail studs, run plates across the tops of the studs, cut rafters for a proper roof pitch, frame up the door and the two windows, shingle my roof and sheath the walls with slab wood. I had a comfortable cabin, a bit smaller than Thoreau's, that served in turn as hideout, print shop, rabbit hutch, auxiliary chicken house, and finally tool shed. The construction skills I learned lasted far longer than the slab-walled cabin that I finally tore down when I went away to college.

Some free association here: Near my cabin my mother housed her large flock of chickens. Each week the *Fricks* truck arrived from Boston to pick up her crates of eggs all sorted by size. Eggs were a mainstay in the Butterfield Farm economy, and had been since my great grandfather's time. Besides the eggs that my mother shipped to Boston, she delivered dozens to stores and households along with the milk and cream produced by our Guernseys. Until gasoline was diverted to the war effort, she made deliveries in a '36 Dodge my father had converted to a delivery van by removing the back seat and trunk. Wartime gasoline rationing ended my mother's deliveries and introduced my own.

My mother was afraid of horses, but my father and I loved them, and stored on a platform above the high mows of the barn there were two disassembled horse carriages, hoisted up there by my grandfather when the automobile came to stay. My father and I brought them down, piece by piece, and put them together again. It was from the two-seated "democrat wagon," with back seat removed, that he, on weekdays, and I, on weekends, delivered milk and eggs through the town. It wasn't fun for man or horse delivering milk in sleet and snow, but a lot of things were inconvenient in wartime. We were lucky to have a couple of sound rigs and a good horse.

After the war my parents bought a pickup, I learned to drive, and life was easy.

For sound reasons I didn't at the time understand, The Log Cabin business was not revived after the war. My father's account book indicates that it was not as flourishing an enterprise as it had seemed to a ten year old. Besides, at war's end my sister married.

12

I have come at last to the end of my guiding wall. Property bounds in the Parmenter era were defined vaguely—"thence northerly on said Gregg's and David Hill Jr.'s land to Silas Hardy's land thence easterly on said Hardy's land to the road leading from the Centre…." I am at the corner of said David Hill, Jr.'s and Silas Hardy's land (as of 1848). No rock cairn marks this corner; even the walls that should meet and mark this corner are missing. This agreed-upon junction is from an era of abutters' mutual trust that only modern surveys have pinpointed and legitimized.

Having traversed some thirty-three acres of Amos Parmenter's original farm, I'm disappointed that the wall along one edge of that acreage just peters out. A hundred feet or more from the exact west end of his farm, the wall simply stops. Did Amos run out of stones? Hardly. They are scattered around. Would a wall here serve no purpose? This corner was likely a long ways from the nearest barn. Besides, the wall that has led me to this spot ends in a swampy area, wet enough that I can find a trickle of water here and there in a dry August. Though it may have seemed impractical to lay up the final few feet of boundary on such unstable land, topography probably figured into the decision to quit wall building here. The recent surveyor's line that marks the end of Parmenter land rests on the face of a precipice above the wetland. Constructing a wall that fills no fencing need against the force of gravity probably didn't make a whole lot of sense. I'm rationalizing my disappointment, I know. What did I expect, an engraved obelisk to reward my long hike?

I have wandered over Parmenter acres divided by purposeful stone walls into three principal portions: North Field, Old Orchard, and Wood/Timber Lot. I have climbed from the level of Parmenter Brook to the base of this steep slope on which lies the west boundary of Amos's farm. I have seen signs of long-ago work and been transported to a boyhood spent on ancestral land. I have witnessed the driving forces of nature. Nature that respects no man's labor. Nature that abhors a piece of fallow land as much as it does a vacuum. Nature that builds up and nature that tears down. But withal, nature that brings memories to life even as it molds its continuing emergence.

In my slow retreat from the woods I come upon a mystery. Deep in the woodlot portion of the Parmenter place there is a wall unlike any I have seen before. It is about sixty feet long, uniformly four feet wide and the customary three feet high. Constructed mostly of stones a man could handily manage, it bespeaks cultivation. Nearby I see the carcass of a bull pine. Such a pine has long limbs growing from the trunk close to the ground, hinting that this tree once grew in the open, and was not competing with any other trees reaching up for sunlight.

This pine put its energy into growing broad rather than tall. It's dead now, but to grow to such a size it lived, perhaps, for a century or more on land which, for at least some number of years, appears to have been regularly cleared of rocks and any competing trees.

Here's the mystery. This solid line of stones connects to no other wall; its ends are at least fifty feet from the nearest boundary. I find no evidence at all that the wall ever served as a fence—no rotted posts, no broken wire ends—and the long, clueless spaces at each end preclude its ever having confined any creatures. Did farmers start a wall at the middle of its length rather than at one of its ends? Perhaps they did, but why wasn't this wall completed, even at one end? As it stands isolated and disconnected in the woods, it makes no sense to me. Why was this land cleared of stones once upon a time? Why were there no competing trees in the vicinity of the bull pine? Everything points to a once-upon-a-time pasture. But a pasture without completed bounds?

Wall as metaphor. Stringing together memories and family stories sparked into consciousness by rocks, water, and trees fools me into thinking I know this place, but there is much more to the lives of the men and women who lived here than I can know.

What little I've learned is like a few stones thrown into the long wall that is my family. So let this lone segment of wall stand unfinished in the woods, a symbol of things known, unknown and to be known about the lives connected to Amos Parmenter's place.

III
Where Parmenter Flows

"In selecting a site in the country, let a lane near your house, grass-grown, cross a sizable brook where is a watering-place."

HENRY DAVID THOREAU

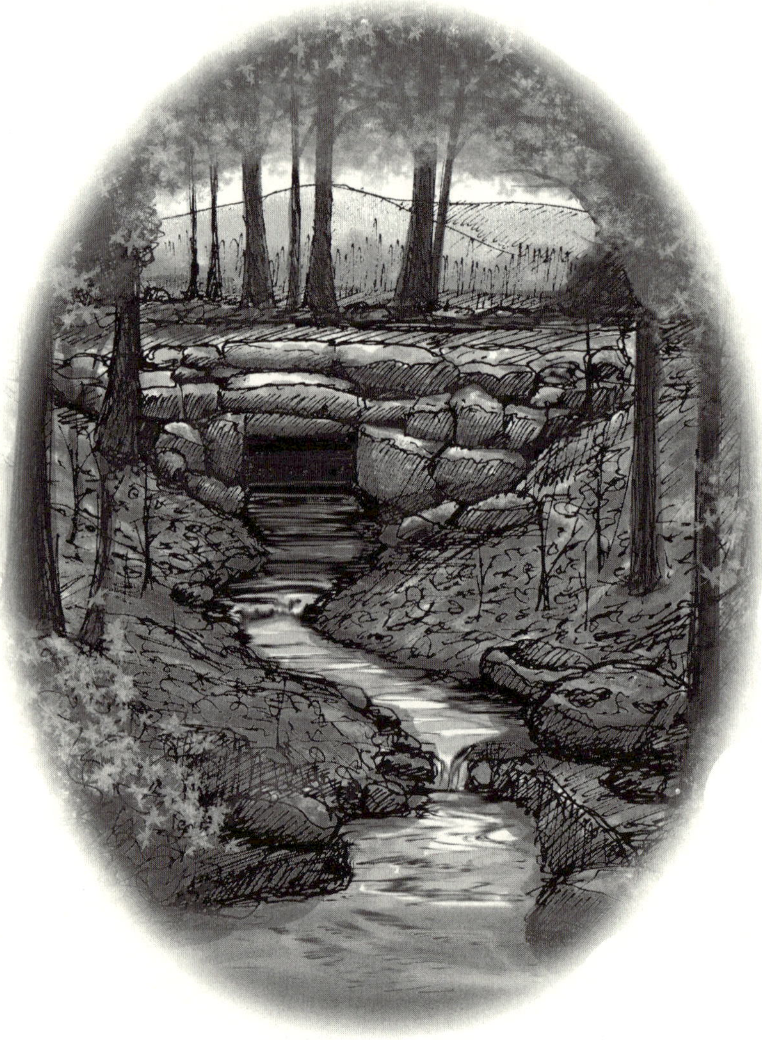

The Fourth of July breaks over my tent with warm sunshine and gentle breezes. I crawl out, stretch the kinks out of my back, and proceed to make the morning's coffee and instant oatmeal. After breakfast, I clean myself up, even shave three days' growth of beard, dig out the one dress shirt I packed and a relatively clean pair of hiking shorts, stick the Stars and Stripes in the outside pocket of my backpack, and in presentable sneakers leave my hermitage for a touch of society. I walk the highway into Antrim Village, called Woodbury's Village in the Parmenter era, for doughnuts and coffee at the bandstand—Antrim's customary Fourth celebration.

I walk anonymously now past houses and shops where everyone knew me seventy-five years ago. I name the families that once occupied the houses I pass—Sawyers, Holts, Hildreths, Kidders, and on and on. I pass Eddie's Store where I ran errands for my grandmother. I stop to remember the rambling complex of red, wooden buildings that housed Abbot Company beside Great Brook. Dozens of men and women manufactured playpens here when I lived in town, but nothing remains of the burned-down factory except its milldam.

In the village I pass my old high school building, now apartments, and the Baptist Church where as a teenager I played the pipe organ for services. Behind the Town Hall I cross over Great Brook on the elegant little footbridge and mingle with the crowd gathering around the bandstand. The coffee is ready, there are homemade sweet rolls, but everyone is waiting for John Robertson to arrive bearing his homemade doughnuts heaped in a washtub. Then the celebration begins.

My nephew, Amos Parmenter's great-great-great-great grandson, and a friend appear in a canoe on Great Brook dressed in colonial costume and wearing tricorns. They climb up the riverbank and arrange themselves before the crowd and begin to read the Declaration of Independence (abbreviated for everyone's sake). As they read, I think about seven-year-old Amos Parmenter and what it must have been like for him to hear these words proclaimed for the first time in Framingham, Massachusetts Bay Colony. I wonder how well the boy understood that what he was hearing meant he was no longer the King's subject, and that from now on he would be an independent *American*. How well did anyone understand what that meant in 1776?

I enjoy being in the midst of a crowd for a little while, but my place is in the Parmenter woods, so, stuffed with doughnuts, I walk the two miles back to my campsite. Early history rules the day, and after changing into my tramping clothes I hike a mile north to the site of the very first village in Antrim.

2

A little north of Amos's cabin, Parmenter Brook marks the arbitrary boundary between two of the several villages that eventually came to make up the township of Antrim. With travel during the town's mid-eighteenth century peopling generally difficult and slow, families gravitated toward more or less independent settlements. Over time Amos Parmenter, who lived into his ninety-seventh year, through the assassination of Abraham Lincoln, witnessed five Antrim villages form and grow up around dam sites, churches, graveyards, schools, and on-again, off-again taverns, stores and post offices.

Atop steep Meetinghouse Hill, about a mile north of Parmenter Brook, are the remains of the oldest of these villages, called in its day "Centor" Antrim (Amos Parmenter's earliest mail was thus addressed, though he lived in the neighboring mill village called, after 1820, Clinton). On the crest of this 1300-foot hill, a mile or so east of the geographic center of the township, a plaque cemented to a boulder marks the site of the original meetinghouse. The "buriing place," laid out in 1777, remains walled in and well-tended beside the marker. An open expanse of land, now privately owned and manicured, gives an idea of what the extensive town commons might have looked like. In its heyday, Centre Antrim boasted eight farmsteads, the meetinghouse and a tavern.

I get a sense of the dynamics of the place from the record of Sarah Hopkins Alld's real estate transactions. Sarah, descending from Scots-Irish, knew a good deal when she saw one. She moved to Centre Antrim from Francestown, New Hampshire, with her near-adult son in 1795, just before Amos arrived and settled a mile down the hill. Sarah had means. She first bought an acre on Meetinghouse Hill in March for six pounds ($30.00), and there she sat. But an acre is not enough land to farm, so in May she "bo't of John McAllester," a bachelor, ten adjacent acres for $40.00, followed in February of 1796 by an additional nine acres acquired from Jonathan Hoyt for $54.00, and finally, on January 6, 1797, she acquired from David Hopkins, who lived across the road from the Christie Tavern on the hill and was about to move to Vermont, five more acres for $40.00. Before she moved on to Cornish, New Hampshire, Sarah owned a goodly portion of Centre Antrim.

Some surmise that the hilltop settlement Sarah called home gave pioneers a measure of security, the elevation providing a natural defense against Native Americans. Tales of atrocities committed by French-allied native braves in some distant parts of New Hampshire during the French and Indian Wars may have influenced farmers to draw together and settle their families on high ground. The year (1744) Philip Riley became the first white man to build a cabin in what was to become Antrim, Native Americans, we're told, drove ten families out of the settlement (now Hillsboro) next down the Contoocook River.

There's archeological evidence that Pennacook tribesmen once fished the Contoocook River where it shapes the east boundary of Antrim, and a few smoked the peace pipe with the first settlers. This reference to Pennacooks is from Reverend John Whiton's *History of the Town of Antrim* (1840):

> *That the territory, now constituting Antrim, was the hunting ground of Indians of the Penacook tribe, and the occasional residence of some of them, is certain. An Indian stone pipe, of neat construction and tastefully ornamented, was found embedded in sand in the crevice of a rock near Esq. Parmenter's, where it has been perhaps for ages.*

How came this pipe to be preserved on Amos's farm so near Meetinghouse Hill, miles from the Pennacook fishing grounds? Did this artifact persuade the settlers that their decision to claim the hilltop had been a judicious one?

My grandmother used to carry our picnic to this ghost village. She explained to me, and the town histories confirm, that "the Old Centor" didn't last long. In 1823, at the instigation of

Amos Parmenter and a few confreres, the town voted to erect a new meetinghouse on the road the villagers had constructed along the southwest brow of Meetinghouse Hill. Over a dozen years, little by little, Centre Antrim moved downhill to a spot a half-mile closer to Parmenter Brook and acquired the slightly more modern name Antrim Center. From the handsome steeple and belfry of Amos's Central Society brick edifice, my grandmother could see Lily Pond, on a summer day aglow with water lilies, and Parmenter Brook sparkling here and there between grassy knolls.

3

Late on such a summer afternoon as this seventy years ago, I would be driving our cows through Parmenter Brook on the way to the barn for milking. The pasture-grass border tamped down by many such crossings has burgeoned into a habitat for birds and small mammals. The scattered shade trees the cows brushed against to rid themselves of flies have been usurped by an exasperating growth of multiflora rose tangled in grapevine. Goldenrod, meadow rue, ironweed and sweet joe-pye weed fill in between clumps of smooth alder as confining as bars in a jail window. Pushing my way through to the stream, I think of the draw, the pull, water has on us.

Approaching Parmenter, I hear it, but I see nothing of it through the dense royal fern. Still it's there and I want to find it. Why? What's so important? Barry Lopez, explorer of the relationship between humanity and nature, writes, "It is through the power of observation, the gifts of eye and ear, of tongue and nose and finger, that a place first rises up in our mind; afterward it is memory that carries the place, that allows it to grow in depth and complexity." So I am drawn here, certainly to listen and to see how it flows today, but chiefly to find what the brook brings to mind. What it awakens.

My room in our farmhouse was the one closest to Parmenter Brook. On summer nights, with the windows open, when I thought of it and tried, I could hear the water falling over rocks and tumbling out of the highway culvert a few hundred feet away. Listening now to the brook lost in weeds, I realize that who I am is partly the effect of what I respond to in my exterior landscape. A little brook may not be much in the way of the world, but here, now, because I attend, it is of moment.

Even when water makes no discernable sound, it draws us to the way it plays with light. Water more than makes up for its colorless property in its reflectiveness. Whose wilderness stroll is not interrupted by the glimpse of bright sky at ground level? Who can ignore the flash of it off a ways through the trees? Who, made aware of some hint of water, is not going to explore to see what more of it there is? Sometimes after heavy rain, a brook will find a fresh route to follow temporarily, and its glitter in new places comes either as a pleasant surprise or a damn nuisance. In the woods, at least, the sight of water is generally a satisfying thing, as now, when I finally see a bit of Parmenter Brook.

Removing boots and socks, I step into the cool water across the field from Amos Parmenter's original cabin site. I am at roughly the midpoint of the stream's full length. The water flowing around my shins has traveled about three-quarters of a mile from glacier-drilled Lily Pond where the brook begins and it will flow downstream of me a bit more than half a mile to its confluence with Great Brook.

But where, in fact, is the midpoint of this stream? United with Great Brook the water will travel a couple of miles to the Contoocook River, then thirty miles or so north and east to the Merrimack, and finally another seventy-five miles south and east to the sea at Newburyport, Massachusetts. Even then, it will not have finished its journey. Energized by the sun, molecules now between my toes will jump off the surface of the ocean and fling themselves into the atmosphere. Rising and dancing invisibly, they'll be caught in air currents and drift in uncountable numbers around the globe and over the hills that ring Lily Pond. There, some will relinquish their energy, coalesce around dust particles and fall as raindrops or snowflakes to the slanted ground and the surface of the pond and begin the long loop again. When, I wonder, were these tickling, chilling molecules here last?

Thinking about the vast travels this water makes by land and sea and air, I'm reminded that Ralph Waldo Emerson says in his essay, *Circles*, "Round every circle another can be drawn; there is no end in nature, but every end is a beginning."

Parmenter Brook as metaphor: Wherever we are, mentally and physically, we are both coming and going. All that has brought us to this place leads us somewhere else.

Right where I'm standing in the brook is proof. I draw a piece of oak branch from the water. The slime that coats it is algae, the same as grew on pulverized rocks submerged here when the last glacier melted. Algae formed the soil mosses grew on, mosses prepared the way for lycopods, lycopods for ferns, and on and on until the brook was flowing through habitat something like the one I'm standing in. Even this is an intermediate stage. They tell us that someday another drastic chill will descend and a glacier will slide over this land, and when it has retreated a new ecosystem will emerge. Circles around circles.

Begin anywhere, with anything, and the brook takes me backwards and forwards from where I am. A frond of wood fern, broken loose upstream, has just floated by me, bobbing on the water's surface, and it takes me back in time, Proustian fashion. There I am, five years old, holding my grandmother's hand as we walk down a gravel road to where this brook flows through a stone culvert. Annie Butterfield picks up a short stick, and leading me to the upstream edge of the overpass, drops it in the water. She hustles me then to the downstream side of the road and we wait. After what seems to me a long time, as if by magic, Grammie's stick floats out into the sunlight and I watch it slowly drift away.

We repeat the trick, with me choosing and tossing twigs, leaves, and fern blades into the water. I watch our little vessels disappear into the dark under the road. I rush to the other side to wait for their sunny arrival. For the next half-dozen years, Parmenter Brook is a favorite playmate.

As I step out of the cold water and find footing on the crowded bank, I'm reminded that where I stand, where I walk on the land, contributes to who I am and how I see the world. This environment is not something that surrounds me merely; it doesn't end at the surface of my skin. It is in me and passes through me. Whatever I attend to is an arc of some circle with me in it. How do I enlarge my sense of circles around circles? What happens to me if I do not?

SEEKING PARMENTER

4

Annie Dillard makes an eloquent argument for observing a stream of water by looking in the direction from which the water is coming. "I look up the creek and here it comes, the future, being borne aloft as on a winding succession of laden trays." Where she stood, Tinker Creek flows over a series of sandstone tiers. "If you look up the creek in any weather, your spirit fills, and you are saying, with an exulting rise of the lungs, 'Here it comes!'. . . There must be something wrong with a creekside person who, all things being equal, chooses to face downstream. It's like fouling your own nest."

My purpose is to watch Parmenter Brook in action, to eavesdrop on the conversation its flowing water makes with the land around it and the air above it, so I will take exception to Dillard and walk *with* the water, inexorably, restlessly down, down as gravity and the land's contours define it. It is in its seaward descent that Parmenter does its work and tells its story. In traveling down from Lily Pond, the brook watered Amos Parmenter's oxen, my grandfather's chickens, my father's milk cows.

To reach Lily Pond, I pass through Center Cemetery laid out across the country highway (NH Route 31) from the site of the handsome edifice Amos built in 1825 (demolished in 1896, victim of demographic shift). Among the many gravestones in Center Cemetery, there are those that mark the patriarch's grave, those of his two wives whom he outlived, and some of his children. My plan is to enter the woods at the base of the cemetery's severe slope and hike for what appears, on my topo map, to be about a thousand feet among trees and glacial erratics until I intercept Parmenter Brook a short distance below Lily

Pond. Once I locate the brook, I'll walk up the stream and thus be able to pinpoint where and how the brook begins. I have not approached Lily Pond by this route before, so yes, like Dillard, I push my way upstream, looking to the water as a bit of future coming at me.

Why am I seeking the brook's precise origin? Why look for Lily Pond at all, since it is not on Amos's farm or even close to its borders? Because it's all connected. The farm could not exist were it not for a reliable watering place. The stream Amos depended on could not exist were it not for a head of water to flow from. The head of water would not exist were it not for a massive glacier having carved its basin. To find Parmenter, man and brook, I follow the water.

Parmenter Brook drops completely out of sight in places, following subterranean channels between great settled boulders. Bright moss on the rocks' upper surfaces suggests where the water may be flowing. Moisture rising through spaces among the rocks provides sufficient water to hydrate the moss and transmit its sperm, and the boulder surfaces provide stable substrate for tenacious moss colonies that adhere with thread-like rhizoids. The aroma of mycorrhizae, fungi within the rhizoids, the same that give freshly-turned soil its fragrance, wafts where moss meets air.

I assumed that in tracking the velvet stones, the color of emerald, and stopping to listen for the water, I could stay in touch with hidden Parmenter Brook until it came to the surface once again. But I was fooled. While I was concentrating on the brook bed running roughly north, Parmenter had, in fact, veered off to the west as a small trickle through ferns I missed completely. The underground water I heard under plush rocks was not Parmenter proper at all, but a tributary stream of vague origin. This false lead did, in the end, take me to the extensive swamp, technically a fen, that surrounds Lily Pond. It gave me my first look at the general source of Parmenter Brook, though the diversion didn't answer to my need to find the brook's beginning. But I was not disappointed. Standing on the muddy edge of acres of blooming water lilies offered reward of its own.

5

There are two distinctly different lilies here. One is the familiar pond lily with its many rows of white, tapering petals and its brilliant egg-yolk center. The ones I am able to reach have a cloyingly sweet scent of almond. The other lily, too far away in the water for me to snag, has yellow petals (actually fleshy sepals, according to my wildflower guide). The blossoms of these bullhead lilies are smaller and not as abundant as the sweet-scented lily, but the two together, hundreds of them, make a dazzling display.

The earliest history of Antrim, written in the 1830s, tells me that, in summer, bushels of water lilies were collected from this site for adorning household parlors and the sanctuary of the meetinghouse. Launching a boat into a quaking swamp in order to harvest lilies was perhaps not the muddy enterprise we might visualize. There probably were then, as there are now, spits of raised, dry land extending to the open water's edge. Given that the swamp spread out to a meadow where cows grazed in early-nineteenth century Antrim Center, it might have been quite a merry excursion on a fine July afternoon for boys to carry a dinghy overland to the water and then row their female companions, equipped with knives and baskets, among the showy flowers.

Henry David Thoreau, wearing his abolitionist's hat, drew encouragement from the contrast between the pristine water lily and its mucky habitat. From his June 16, 1854, journal entry:

> *Again I scent the white lily, and a season I had waited for has arrived. How indispensable all these experiences to make up the summer. It is the emblem of purity, and its scent suggests it. Growing in stagnant and muddy water, it bursts up so pure and fair to the eye and so sweet to the scent, as if to show us what purity and sweetness reside in and can be extracted from the slime and muck of earth.... What confirmation of our hopes is in the fragrance of the water-lily! I shall not so soon despair of the world for it, notwithstanding slavery, and the cowardice and want of principle of the North. It suggests that the time may come when man's deed will smell as sweet.*

I know what he means. Looking out on this extraordinary display, my worldly concerns fly off to Mars. I have never been this close to so dense a growth of water lilies. It is as if I could walk across the dazzle. As it is, I step away from the muddy edge and push my way through the dense growth along the northern quarter of the pond's perimeter, jotting down names as I go.

My tree inventory includes red maple (also aptly named swamp maple), black oak, white oak, yellow birch, black cherry, beech, white pine, eastern hemlock, and red spruce. Such a variety of deciduous and evergreen trees says to me that I walk on rich soil, conducive once to grassy meadows where Amos Parmenter might well have summer-pastured his young stock.

By far my most exciting tree find is a stand of mature American Chestnut trees (*Castanea dentata*). This tree species was wiped out in the eastern United States by Japanese chestnut bark disease early in the twentieth century. Today most chestnuts east of the Mississippi attain only shrub height before the fungus, still in the soil, kills them. I have scrambled through many stands of doomed chestnuts sprouting. But only a few yards back from Lily Pond's edge there are chestnut trees thirty feet tall bearing green fuzzy burs at the tips of their upper branches. I will return in the fall to collect some ripe nuts before bears take them all. Claw scratch marks on the trunks of the chestnut trees let me know I will have competition.

Among the shrubs I can identify: low sweet and high bush blueberry (ripe in another week or so), huckleberry, blackberry, leatherleaf, lambkill (which is, as the name implies, poisonous to livestock), and goosefoot maple. The wildflowers I know by name include blue flag growing in the shallow water with cattail, and on the drier edge, sedges, bunchberry, meadowsweet, pitcher plant and round-leaved sundew.

These latter two are insectivorous plants at home in peatland. Pitcher plants trap and digest insects in a vase formed by modified leaves. Sundews catch their food by luring unsuspecting flies and things to their sweet, gluey leaves and enfolding them as digestive enzymes go to work. I spend some time watching these unusual plants secure their midday meal.

Bracken fern flourish a little way back from the water. Because its rhizomes (ferns don't have true roots) grow deep in the soil, this plant can survive landscape disturbances that wipe out other ferns. Bracken is often a sign of former pasture (though some say the mature plant contains cyanide and is poisonous to cattle). Even when pastures grow into forests and the forests are cut over, the tough bracken fern survives. So I take the presence of these bracken as corroborating evidence that cattle once grazed where I am forcing my way through shrubs and trees.

After a short rest following my waterside botanizing, and fortified with a granola bar, I venture out on the long beaver dam that runs across the eastern rim of the fen. Picking my way carefully, one eye on my footing and the other on the expanse of peatland water I might easily come to know intimately, I arrive eventually at a point where I can confirm what I expected—that the pond and its surrounding fen are two nearly separate bodies of water. An aerial photo of Lily Pond shows, and now I can see for myself, the topographical relationship of the pond to its surrounding and extensive fen. While the swamp is completely carpeted with lily pads and blossoms and punctuated by snags of drowned hemlock, the surface of Lily Pond itself is entirely devoid of any macroscopic plant life. I surmise that the pond is too deep for water lily or any other aquatic plant to take root. The sharp demarcation of the pond's rim abundantly marked by a berm of leatherleaf and blueberry (confirmed on a winter walk across the ice) is convincing of the water's depth. As well, while the fen is dotted with beaver lodges, both abandoned and active, none appear in the profound pond. Lily Pond proper is an island of very deep water in a shallow sea of swamp flora and fauna.

Teetering on this massive beaver dam, I have to remind

myself that when Amos Parmenter visited Lily Pond there were no beaver dams or lodges here at all. The beaver-pelt market had proven so lucrative in the century before Amos came to Antrim that the animals had been all but extirpated in New Hampshire by 1800. He looked out on a vastly different scene. Without beaver work there would have been much less water in the peatland, and the edges of the swamp would have been much contracted compared with what I see. I look over many acres of open water; he saw fewer acres and those thick with soggy moss.

Lily Pond began as a kettle hole. Ten thousand years ago or more a huge calf of ice at the edge of the receding glacier broke off, and an outwash of loose rock fragments, called till, buried it. When the giant ice block finally melted it left a deep depression amid the rocks. Crushed bedrock deposited by tons of melting and slowly receding ice formed a more or less level rock field around the deep hole. Water from the melted ice filled the depression and the excess flooded into the rock debris, in due course cultivating a perfect habitat for hydrophytes, most abundantly *Sphagnum* moss.

At Lily Pond (the name applies to both the deep water and the shallow peatland), the slowly decaying moss held the water in saturated, acidic and anaerobic soil that discouraged an overgrowth of trees. Organic matter, accumulating over centuries, its decay slowed by the acid conditions, formed a yards-thick mat, the peat, atop the rock debris and stagnant water surrounding the kettle. Early settlers referred to the hazardous result as a quaking bog. "Cattle caught in the mud here are said to sink very slowly yet surely out of sight," warns Antrim's first historian.

Whether or not Amos Parmenter ever watched helplessly as his heifer sank out of sight, the moss was important to him.

Sphagnum is a large moss, as mosses go, its stems sometimes an inch wide and over a foot in length. Its water-retaining biomass was important to Amos, but so was another *Sphagnum* feature: The moss takes up and stores calcium. It is this fact of bryophytic physiology that creates the Parmenter connection. Amos and his neighbors farmed in soil made of pulverized granite, a calcium-poor rock. To replace the essential mineral that his crops drew from the soil, Amos relied on peat moss.

An excerpt from the earliest history of Antrim:

> *Little Pond* [now Lily Pond], *half a mile south-west from the centre, has a surface of only some half dozen acres. It is bordered in part by a shaking bog; as you recede a little from the water, the bog becomes drier and firmer, and spreads into a meadow, overlaying a deep substratum of peat or swamp mud, an article of which there are tens of thousands of cords, and which is valued as an important ingredient in compost manure. This substance, with proper management and intermixture, is capable of enriching all the adjacent farms.* (ca. 1840)

For some distance into the backed-up water, I walk on a line of rocks laid down two centuries ago. Resembling an underwater stone fence, I suspect these rocks are what remain of a barrier constructed to steer any flowing water into a channel. Ignoring the extensive beaver construction that has occurred since and now partially obscures it, I see that the original stonework was an engineering project of no low order. By directing the runoff water that flowed through the mossy mat into a valley, the farmers were attempting to put the peatland under "proper management."

SEEKING PARMENTER

There was benefit in regulating the depth of the water. This becomes obvious at the stone dam, some seventy-five yards downgrade and east of the retaining wall. I can see that the wall guides the water into a natural, cutaway funnel created by ledge outcropping on one side and a high, stable hillock on the other. At the narrow end of the funnel the farmers took control.

To block the funnel, they constructed a water gate of huge angular stones that they maneuvered into place around a square opening at the bottom of their dam. Thick silting prevents me from finding evidence of whatever kind of gate they devised across the opening. To get an idea of the depth of the accumulated silt, I measure the distance from the top of the rock dam to the surface of flowing water. On the downstream side, the height is nearly five feet. On the upstream (pond) side, only eighteen inches separates the top rocks from the surface of the silt. Thus, to see more of the controlled opening I would have to remove three feet of underwater sediment—tempting, but impractical. It doesn't take a great leap of imagination, however, to picture the farmers at an appointed time hammering their gate into place and backing the water up into the quaking bog and meadow.

It is my conjecture that the stone structure was planned and with considerable expenditure of time and energy put in place so that periodically the meadow could be flooded to create more swamp muck, essentially accomplishing what the present beaver dam does. In the fall of the year, the gate would be raised and the swamp water drawn down. Come winter, with the ground frozen hard enough to walk on, the farmers could plow up the brown gold and fill their wagons. I suspect Amos Parmenter was among those making trips here. It may have been his oxen that dragged the great stones into place to build the water gate. In turn, he was likely one of the farmers reaping the benefit. I do not doubt that he bent his back to the arduous task of harvesting good compost to fertilize his fields with calcium-rich peat oxcarted from Lily Pond.

In his *Walden* chapter, "The Pond in Winter," Thoreau gives a description of peat harvesting. It was done in winter, presumably before there was deep snow to contend with. Using ox-drawn plows, the farmers opened up the gelid peat bed as if they were preparing to plant a crop. Then with their drill-barrows, turf-knives, spades, saws, rakes and with a double-pointed pike-staff Thoreau had never seen before, they "began to hook up the virgin mould itself, with a peculiar jerk, clean down to the sand, or rather the water . . . and haul it away on sleds." Thoreau watched as gangs of a hundred men harvested the peat and shipped it off by train (1846).

I doubt that Antrim farmers operated on anything like such a scale. Thoreau's description, though, helps me picture an activity I might have witnessed some winter days along the edges of Lily Pond a couple of centuries ago.

Even if my picture of what went on here is not entirely accurate, the stone structure is nevertheless an impressive human artifact. I look on these sharp edges, the angular facets of these great rocks, and see what Amos saw. I study the arrangement of the rocks that have withstood two centuries of ice and water pressure and know it was my ancestor or his close neighbors who drew them here and maneuvered them into place; who then stood back and admired their handiwork; who supposed that what they had made would be of service to men well beyond their own time. In a sense, those farmers were thinking of me. They could not imagine I would have no need of Lily Pond peat.

Nor would they have imagined what a struggle it is for me to get across the beaver dam and through the dense brush and high hemlocks to photograph their construction. What they did suppose, though, is that I, or someone like me, would come here one day and appreciate what they had made. There must have been some satisfaction in that.

It is for me to grant their satisfaction. I feel privileged to have such an opportunity. It feels as though by my standing beside their work, taking my notes and triggering my camera, I am honoring them. That feels good.

What feels equally good is my own satisfaction that I have found Parmenter Brook at its source. It trickles through the silt-filled channel, flows down the constructed exit and begins its drop to the sea right here.

6

This is as good a place as any to interrupt the Parmenter story to explain my frequent references to Henry David Thoreau. It is my sense that the Parmenters (Amos's son George was Thoreau's exact contemporary) represent the social order that the Transcendentalist anti-materialist was so critical of. The Parmenters were ambitious people determined to get ahead in any way they could. America was, they had no doubt at all, the land of opportunity. Cutting down trees, ripping up soil, damming streams, carving out roads hither and yon to speed communication, buying and selling land to their good advantage—the Parmenters pushed and pulled from dawn to dusk to make a buck.

Thoreau took it upon himself to point out the error in such worship of commerce and labor. Though he didn't know them personally, he might have viewed men like Amos and George Parmenter this way: "Most men, even in this comparatively free country, through mere ignorance and mistake, are so occupied with the factitious cares and superfluously coarse labors of life that its finer fruits cannot be plucked by them. Their fingers, from excessive toil, are too clumsy and tremble too much for that. . . . The finest qualities of our nature, like the bloom on fruits, can be preserved only by the most delicate handling."

No isolated quote can do justice to the complex man Thoreau was—a scold, yes, but also mountain hiker, ecologist, agitator, abolitionist, lecturer and essayist. Likewise, no crop field that Amos Parmenter cleared from forest can stand adequately for a man who founded a church, administered his town's affairs for many years, and represented Antrim in the state legislature.

Though contemporaries, the world just looked different to them. Parmenter's view was chiefly agrarian and entrepreneurial. For him nature was a commodity and wildness a curse, and it was a man's holy obligation to tame what he could. For Thoreau: "How near to good is what is *wild!*"

Today I'm more in sympathy with Thoreau (my distant cousin) than I am with Parmenter (my great-great-great-grandfather). Had I lived among them, who knows?

The point I like to keep in mind, and the reason Thoreau's commentary accompanies me where I walk, is that there were these two streams of thought about the natural world—one utilitarian, one reverential—running parallel in nineteenth-century New England. Ironically, while the utilitarian view was always predominant, as it is today, the New England countryside is richer now in wildness than it was when Thoreau and Parmenter walked over this land. Today commercial enterprise is concentrated in cities while moose, bear, coyote and wild turkey roam through grown-over farms.

Would I rather be striding loosely through Amos's open pasture than scrambling through the jumbled second growth that occupies his land? No. I'm happy experiencing this stage of ecological succession. Something is going on here that is largely independent of human influence (though not wholly, for sure), and it makes me curious. It causes me to keep asking, "What next?" And in that I am like both Thoreau and the Parmenters who must have always wondered what would emerge from their setting.

7

Moving downstream from the stone dam, I picture Amos Parmenter walking along the brook from his church to his farm on a Sunday afternoon. Not his most direct route, to be sure, but one that afforded him a chance to assess the land and its productivity. But how different the scene was then compared to what I look on. The boulders along the stream were in full light when he was last here. They were not upholstered in shade-tolerant moss, but in crusty lichen flourishing in bright sun. Forage smoothed the rise and fall of the land under his feet where I trip over brush. Sheep and cow paths curved around the slopes. The scent of ripening grasses, not the fragrance of hemlocks, filled his nose. Where I hear the *teacher-teacher-teacher* of an ovenbird in the thick woods, he heard the cooing of passenger pigeons, extinct now, but sky-darkeningly common in his day. The sound of a lawn mower in the distance replaces the sheep bells he would have been listening for. This stream that merely excites my curiosity he approached as a thing vital to his way of life.

The color of Parmenter. Just below its rock-strewn beginning, the brook fills a pool, maybe three feet deep with water so densely colored I cannot see the bottom. Its surface is frothy with swirling, water-whipped glutinous exudate of hemlocks. Further along, after the water leaves the pool, it enters shallows. The froth dissipates and I can see the gravel bottom, stained a rich gold by tannin tea, the contribution of crushed, steeped hemlock bark. Much further along, where it meanders among swamp reeds, its surface acquires an iridescent purple sheen. In an open field it reflects the sky's blue and its wavelets glitter in the sun. Parmenter's water has no color of its own, so it borrows from its habitat.

"The field of water betrays the spirit that is in the air. It is continually receiving new life and motion from above. It is intermediate in its nature between land and sky." When Thoreau penned those words he issued no ominous warning. Applied to Parmenter's source and to the brook I follow today, Thoreau's words assume a prophetic tone different from the celebratory spirit in which they were uttered.

What strikes me as I walk beside the open brook is how vacant the water is. Colored its surface and gravel base may be here and there, but the water itself appears nearly empty. Little lives in the brook. I see none of the fish, brookies, I once fed on. I find not a single frog where seventy years ago I caught a dozen in an afternoon. Aquatic insects that used to crowd Parmenter's quiet surfaces are only scattered now. Aside from the occasional orange newt, there are few other vertebrates or invertebrates visible to the stream-wanderer's eye. Absence signals acidified precipitation. "Water betrays the spirit that is in the air."

I was surprised to learn from Bill McKibben's *End of Nature* that knowledge of acid rain is not new. As long ago as when Amos's son George was cutting firewood to heat his big house, English observers had connected acid water to smoke from coal-burning plants. It took a long time for the acid-rain issue to reach the level of public concern it has now, because it was and is difficult to make an argument for reducing air pollutants no one actually sees, McKibben explains.

Parmenter Brook, as it has been before, is under pressure to adapt to new conditions. I worry that the brook's broader ecology is being altered by acidic rain and snow. Parmenter's water has been acidic ever since the peatland developed at Lily Pond, and habitats along its bank have adapted, but now come nitrous oxides from engine exhaust and sulfur and carbon oxides from coal fires and petro fuels to lower pH and compromise the plants.

Agronomists know that acidic precipitation leaches minerals such as calcium and magnesium from the soil. Amos Parmenter's granitic loam is low in calcium and magnesium to begin with. Botanists have shown that deprived of these crucial minerals, eastern hemlock trees, the species that in places crowds Parmenter's course, are stunted. Entomologists are quick to point out that harmful insects do more extensive damage to trees under stress than they do to healthy specimens. I am looking for signs of damage as I go. I don't see evidence that the hemlocks blocking my way downstream are under attack or weakened in any way, but knowing that they could be, I inspect the lower branches, looking on the underside of twigs for the cottony egg masses of the woolly adelgid, a sap-sucking threat invading New Hampshire.

Where hemlocks give way to maples and birch, I'm on the lookout for telltale clusters of half-inch exit holes drilled by Asian longhorn beetles, another recent destructive invader of the New England woods. I don't find any as far up the trunks as I can see, but I keep looking, because some tree species are more resistant to this insect's damage than others. Cherry and alder, both of which I encounter on the stream bank, are not good hosts for longhorns, but maple and birch, also here, are. So, if the longhorn moves into these woods, the forest landscape Parmenter Brook knows today may change with sickened maples giving way to resistant alder. Who but I will care?

Who but this sojourning bushwhacker regrets this kind of ecological succession? Who but this short-lived wanderer has the audacity to make value judgment on what happens in the ageless wild? What other species but my own has the capacity to concern itself with the forest's future? Or its past?

I travel along with this water as it moves in and out of various forest communities and I'm reminded that long before Amos Parmenter had his say about what transpired here habitats evolved. I see ahead of me a few red spruce trees mixed among taller white pines. But paleobotanists tell me these species did not emerge together on this post-glacial terrain. Spruce pollen resides lower down in lake-bottom core samples than does pine pollen, so spruces were here first, 10,000 years ago compared to 9,000 years for white pine. Hemlock appeared a thousand years after white pine, and American beech followed hemlock by 1500 years. I walk under all these species, each apparently satisfied with the growing conditions that exist now, but knowing that they appeared serially, I can't help wondering if they will disappear in some similar sequence if acidic precipitation differentially increases some trees' susceptibility to insect damage and plant disease.

The one thing I can count on is that succession will happen. Something will emerge from what is around me now. Circles around circles, says Emerson. There is no end to nature.

8

What may happen here someday is not what piques my curiosity at the moment I step into a two-foot deep pool. What intrigues me is the varying volume of water Parmenter appears to carry. Here a full brook rushes rambunctiously around me; there I lose the subdued and lazy trickle in thick ferns. I come to broad shallow washes, and then I find deep pools like this one holding hundreds of gallons. How is it that the amount of water, which must be more or less constant, appears to differ from place to place? In addition to obstructions that pocket the water here and there, the variation in the porosity of the underlayment and the bank material must account for this range of water volume and enthusiasm. In places where soil particles are large and gravelly, water runs through the interstices and much of it disappears from sight. Somewhere else impenetrable hardpan and bedrock force water to the surface, and I see all there is of it. Besides differences in the structure of the earth lying under the brook, bank material varies as well. Where soft and sandy, Parmenter sinks in; where hard, Parmenter piles up or floods over. While I am fascinated by these variable dynamics, they are only superficial phenomena. Parmenter's serious endeavor to reach the sea does not waver along its course.

I don't recall that the volume of Parmenter Brook was of any great concern to my dairy-farming father. As long as the brook flowed—and it never dried up—there was water for his cows. A milking cow imbibes a prodigious amount of water—upwards of thirty-five gallons a day. I understood that emphatically when it was necessary to deliver water to Bossy by the pailful.

In winter, when the cows were in the barn, they drank from watering cups connected to pipework that carried spring water. With her nose Bossy depressed a grill within the drinking cup and water gushed in. As a boy it intrigued me that a cow, new to the device, seemed immediately to know how to work it—when it worked. Frozen pipes in the wintry barn meant I had to ferry pails and pails of water to the cows from an in-barn concrete cistern through which we allowed water to slowly flow so that it wouldn't freeze. In summer, when the cows stayed outdoors both day and night, returning to the barn only at milking times, Parmenter Brook supplied their water. There was no other source.

Out of idle curiosity I decide to set up a station to measure the stream's rate of flow and see just how much water the brook brings to the farm. First I find a straight section of the brook. The longest straight stretch I find is fifteen feet. At each end I measure the width and then the depth at one-foot intervals across the stream. Multiplying width times depth at each end and averaging the results yields a virtual slice of water 46.7 square feet in cross section. A piece of orange peel timed as it floats on the surface from one end to the other indicates that the water slice moves through fifteen feet in 171 seconds, translating to a rate-flow of thirty-six gallons per second, more than Bossy would drink in a whole day and night. No wonder we never worried about the cows going thirsty.

9

I come now to what remains of a stone-constructed culvert, the brook's first man-made impediment to its flow since falling out of Lily Pond. Heavy, layered and fitted stones suggest that they shored up a roadbed, but nothing of the road itself remains. Its reasoned route is written over by tall rock maples and red oaks. Beneath the trees, sawed stumps, hemlock I judge, tell me that another sentence was laid down earlier. Much had been written in the land before this road came and after it went. When town roads, often little better than blazed trails through the woods, were "given up," they disappeared with barely a trace. Only where the path encountered running water was any lasting construction involved. If there was ever a road here, it was discontinued long, long ago, written over, leaving this collapsed memorial.

As much as I would like this account of Parmenter Brook to be a naturalist's-eye view, I am drawn more to the human artifacts in the woods than to the ecological relationships that I know, in theory, are working themselves out on this abandoned farmland along the stream. Two reasons: One, I am not expert enough in forest biology to give detailed accounts of all that I am seeing. Biological relationships in these woods are more complex than my casual sightings reveal. I am left, then, with the sensuousness that comes with walking this brook, only part of the time augmented by what I know about woods and field ecology. Often I walk along looking and feeling and sniffing, and forgetting all about the field guides I carry on my back.

The other reason my walk beside Parmenter is not strictly biological is that the human use of this land is never far from my mind. When I see a dozen rocks stacked up or deliberately laid down in a pattern anywhere in these woods, the intention preceding their arrangement crowds my thinking. Amos Parmenter, or someone like him, was here. He had a purpose in mind for these rocks, and for a time that purpose took precedence over his other concerns. I cannot walk past his structures and not think of him. I am compelled to fathom his designs, as I am not that of the wild, because I am more kin to him than to wildness. He was of another time, but he reasoned, he planned, he applied his energy as I do to accomplish ends. The wildness happening around me, on the other hand, has no end purpose, no *teleos*. What is going on in the wild makes its ends as it executes its means. There is no design in wildness, only correlation. With one of Amos's stone or log structures, the end was in mind before the work began. I am out here puzzled by those ends, and thus connected to him whose ends they were.

Once out of the forgotten culvert, Parmenter Brook drops steeply again. Where it falls this time it disappears between boulders, gurgling like a jug being emptied. The water evidently drops still deeper underground, because I hear a muffled, higher pitched sound, a complement to the first, coming up through crevices. Parmenter is singing both soprano and alto parts of a duet about its journey and how, though it has been going on for eons, it seems new each minute. Every spill between rocks feels fresh, as though it has never happened before. Each penetration into the dark spaces between rocks is a new adventure. To flow is to be always discovering.

One of the finest spots along Parmenter is not far downstream from the singing. Where the water encounters flattened terrain, the brook is as silent as the grass growing beside it, as silent as the sunlight feeding the grass. In this brief interval, no trees cast shade on land or water. Here is a tiny oasis of bright meadow in the forest. After the grassy interlude comes the sunny, exposed ledge, and Parmenter spreads out a thin sheet of water over the gently tilted and terraced granite slabs. Aquatic moss carpets the stone surface, nearly covering the tiered rock with a loden green mat swaying in the broad waters, its pile tinged with deepest red. Though now in summer I watch Parmenter move leisurely, languidly, over the stones, I imagine that in spring there must be a forceful torrent of runoff rushing across these surfaces, yet the tenacious moss, likely a species of *Fontinalis*, persists. It was growing when Amos visited this place and probably long before.

Moss is about as versatile a plant as nature has contrived. Being simple in structure, without flowers or true leaves, stems or roots, and most species reaching less than an inch in height, moss finds accommodations on boulders, tree bark, and even old bones. A living moss needs at least a thin film of water clinging to it. Morning dew will suffice. Moss plants depend on this enveloping moisture for the necessary exchange of gases with the air and to keep their cells plumped and working. The same meager water film allows for the dispersal of sperm, too. Because moss can reproduce both sexually by spores and asexually by cloning, one species or another manages to propagate in a wide range of microhabitats from the severely arid to, as on this water-washed ledge, perpetual inundation.

Along Parmenter, where ferns, grasses or other herbaceous plants don't crowd them out, dozens of the many species of moss brighten my walk. Where I look down on a uniform carpet of moss, a bryophytologist would identify dozens of species sharing the same surface. Even I notice, for instance, that the type of moss growing on the butt end of a fallen tree, the colonies two feet above ground level, is different from the species growing on the nearly buried branches. Like me, these woodland mosses love the cool, moist and shady places.

10

Not far downstream from the ledge steps I come to the first of five stone walls Parmenter Brook will pass through. This one, more clearly than some of the others, shows a phenomenon familiar to those who explore the New England woods. Caught on the upstream side of the wall, sticks, leaf debris and silt have built up the ground so that the capstones of the wall are less than a foot above the ground surface. When I step over the wall, the ground drops out from under me, and the wall stands three feet high or more. Ever since Amos or one of his neighbors constructed this wall, Parmenter has been depositing litter against it as it sieved through the rocks. It has swept away the debris from the downstream side and carried it to the next obstacle it comes to. In some places the heavy stones are completely buried. Every fallen, hidden wall that crosses the stream is witness to Parmenter Brook's labors.

Sometimes woods ecology changes abruptly at a stone wall. The second stone wall Parmenter encounters in its run from Lily Pond separates an area filled with young hardwood trees, nothing over eight inches in diameter, from huge pines and hemlocks two feet across as measured four and a half feet from the ground. On the upstream side of the wall I am warmed by the sun filtering through a thin canopy of young maples, ash, black and silver birch, and red oaks. I see a few stumps of harvested pine and hemlock scattered among the young trees. Not too many years ago this area was cut over and the mature trees removed for lumber. The tree harvesting created holes in the canopy and seedlings of hardwoods took advantage of the penetrating sunlight.

I learned from forest biologist Bernd Heinrich that the smaller the seeds of a tree species are, maple for example, the more crucial it is that they germinate in a sunny spot so that the seedling tree can begin right away to make its own food. Trees like beech and oak that grow from nuts containing a good supply of food are able to propagate and develop even where the canopy shades the germinating plant. In this upstream, upwall woods, a variety of trees found conditions just right for germinating and developing. All around me a new hardwood forest is in the making.

What I see happening here tells me that as pine forests are harvested, hardwoods will replace the softwoods where the conditions are right. Unless reforestation is deliberately managed to cultivate conifers, or the taking of mature pines is done selectively, the vistas from New Hampshire hilltops may be quite different down the years from what we climb to see today, especially in autumn when hardwoods are in full glory—less forest green, more red, yellow and orange.

I step over the wall and am immediately in dark, cooling shade. There are some mature maples and ash trees contributing to the canopy, but chiefly I am walking under scented evergreens. Only a scattering of chestnut, ironwood and hobblebush saplings reaching for the scant sunlight fill in under the mature timber. I can see across the forest for a considerable distance.

This open setting beneath tall trees reminds me that the Native Americans of New England made a fall practice of burning the woods. Fire did little harm to the tough-barked adult trees, but it thinned the undergrowth of saplings so that braves could see deer through the open woods, and their arrows were more likely to strike food than tree trunk. Fire encouraged browse to sprout to feed game animals. Burning up dry branches on the ground meant moccasin-shod feet could walk silently into firing range of a buck. Where I go, snapping twigs with every footfall, I cannot help making my presence known to wildlife. A blue jay tells me so.

In the dark woods I discover a large maple felled by a stiff wind some years ago. The thick trunk broke with the fall. The stump is swarming with winged insects, possibly wood wasps of some kind, every body in touch with two or three others, the black mass streaming over the decayed wood. (Wood wasp larvae bore into dead and decaying wood of deciduous trees and live there for a year or two. I may have witnessed a mass molting of adults.) Tremulous wings like sequins shimmering in candlelight catch the weak sun filtering through the dense canopy. The wasps, if they are that, are concentrated on the stump. Only a scattered few crawl along the still bark-covered trunk. There is something nutritious, probably energy-rich fungus, in the rotting wood. I watch this moving sheet of insects for a long time, but so lost are they in their work they pay no attention to me. The shadow cast over them by my waving hand disturbs them not at all. I am so fascinated by this spread of insects that it does not occur to me to collect specimens in order to make a positive identification later.

Here, too, I find a white ash tree, a foot in diameter, dead yet still erect. It has been almost completely girdled about one-and-a-half feet from the ground. Because the exposed wood bears no deep teeth gouges such as beaver create, I suspect a wandering porcupine seeking nutritious tree sap did the deed. This was lethal damage since the food a tree makes and lives on travels though a thin layer of phloem just inside the outer bark. Gnawing away that critical tissue dooms the tree to death by root starvation.

Beginning underground the tree died an inch at a time. Still it stands. Not today, but one day this ash will fall and become part of the forest floor. Bacteria will break down its cell walls and free its stored minerals, fungi will suck up its nutrients, insects will devour the wood for the fungi, and worms and mice will recycle the remains of insects, fungi and cellulose fibers into forest soil. An ash seed from a living neighbor may fall into the rich compost and germinate, giving the life cycle another turn. But not yet.

I knock on the standing corpse to see if I can startle flying squirrels from their nest inside a hole left where a limb broke off. That happened once. I was in the woods leading an ecology field trip when we came to a tree like this one. As I talked to the group about the utility of dead trees, I hit the tree with my hand. Out of a limb hole near the top, three flying squirrels flung out the extensible folds of skin along their sides and glided to a tree nearby. Flying squirrels are nocturnal, but that day we got to see these startled, bug-eyed creatures in broad daylight. For twenty years I have been knocking on dead trees. In twenty years no flying squirrel has appeared, and none sailed out today. But who's to say that it won't happen sometime? Like a persistent dog that has learned to sit up and beg at the table from a single successful try, such as the morning he got a piece of bacon, just that one time, when he sat up on his haunches, I go about knocking on dead trees.

I wander upslope about a hundred feet from Parmenter Brook to rest in the shade of tall evergreens undisturbed for a great many years. If trees were ever harvested here, it was a long time ago. No stumps protrude through the thick, soft duff, though ubiquitous granite chunks lie scattered. It is dark and cool where I am, but in the distance the brook sparkles in full, warming sunlight. The contrasting conditions impress me and start me thinking that the flashing stream says more emphatically than maturing timber or eroding granite can that to be is to change. I receive this lesson from the wild and allow it to enter my consciousness, and thus I make response to what the brook teaches me. We are in communication, the brook and I. My inner landscape is enriched. How could I not be changed?

Once again the ecology shifts dramatically as I step over the third stone wall. This one, too, has collapsed where Parmenter has undermined it. A minute ago I was on dry land under huge pines and hemlocks, now I am in full sun, in a swale thick with ferns as high as my chest. I am amid bracken with its nearly horizontal fronds, coarse-bladed sensitive fern, shaggy-rachised interrupted fern, and delicate New York fern. Here and there I trip over rocks I cannot see through the lush growth around my feet. Though my boots are in shallow, iridescent water, Parmenter is mostly contained in a channel along the south side of a recently mowed field that slopes down from higher, dryer land to this soggy flat.

This boggy patch of cattails and blue flag owes its luxuriance to an old agricultural enterprise, Bass Farm, formerly Pastor Whiton's place. Since the days of the good reverend, runoff from the large field, sometimes bearing manure, peat compost and the residue from seeding and mowing, has fed this saturated land along its lower edge. So while this abundance of reeds, sedges, grasses and wildflowers is wild, it has benefited from its close proximity to small-scale agribusiness. Shall we call the rich runoff pollution or manna?

To the south, directly across Parmenter Brook from the mowed field and its flowery mire, I come upon an area of open water. Some years ago, I judge, beaver partially dammed the water, though Parmenter continues to flow uninhibited along its northern edge. While the dam is obvious, and in need of repair, there is no beaver lodge and not a single tree snag stands in this water. The rim of the flowage bears a canopy of alder, ash and red maple, but evidence of beaver activity is scant. Perhaps beaver started to settle here but were unsettled when a new house appeared and a lawn came to occupy the land that

Parmenter now waters as it once watered cropland and, before that, forest.

Lost in my thoughts about the transformations Parmenter has witnessed along its banks, I am pleasantly surprised by one small, relaxed beaver swimming in quiet circles, coming as close as ten feet from me. At no time does it slap its broad tail, or dive out of sight. It appears to be quite contented in my presence. I decide that this beaver is probably migrating from an active colony in search of suitable habitat attracted, maybe, by cattails growing in abundance in the pond. Its quiet demeanor, lacking any indication of territoriality, suggests that this impoundment is not this beaver's permanent home.

Beaver kits stay with their parents for two years. Then if the home pond is small or food too far afield, the two-year-old migrates to new habitat. It looks to me as if this beaver might be house hunting. But this is not the place. I draw my conclusion from the fact that this pond is not two hundred feet from an occupied house and attendant traffic, hardly the most auspicious location for an active beaver colony. I look around for a beaver's favorite food—poplars and cottonwood, ash and sugar maple in a pinch—but find none. Only two small black birch trees have been gnawed. The dry stems indicate that the stumps are a few weeks old. Since both birches are hung up in other trees, their leaves desiccated, the beaver received no nutritious benefit from its labors, though chipping away at the trunks honed its huge incisors. All in all, I suspect this young beaver will soon move elsewhere, though I think he enjoys spending a few minutes with me.

In a little less than half its full length, Parmenter Brook

falls out of Lily Pond, traverses cutover woods, a long-undisturbed forest, a mowed field, a marsh, and skirts a beaver pond. It crosses under ATV bridges and passes through three stone walls. Nearly everywhere—Bass Farm swale the exception—Parmenter is shaded by tall trees.

Two hundred years ago Amos and his neighbors pushed the forest back from the stream. The slopes were smooth and green. Belled, curious sheep flocked together, bleating to any farm boy passing within sight. Young heifers watched to see if he was bringing salt, and the milk cows, munching their cuds, swiveled their huge heads to follow his movement. In the distance the boy heard the rumble of an oxcart or the clip of horse hooves on the gravel road. The air, though he wouldn't have noticed it, smelled of manure and wood smoke. Dogs barked at the Parmenter place.

11

Not unlike the way the long wall changes character in places, Parmenter Brook alters its personality as it flows. It is as if it feels its state of being—voluble here, sedate there, liberated here, confined there. Just below the beaver pond, the brook is tamed by new construction beside it. A long driveway leads to a new house, and Parmenter is forced into a two-foot diameter, black plastic conduit to pass under the roadway. But once free of the confining polystyrene, Parmenter shows new vigor. It seems excited. It runs faster. It breaks into streamlets that dance around little islands crowned with alders. It bends and weaves through the overgrowth of weeds and ferns. Anticipation is in the air and water.

Still under tall trees, the brook edges another house lot, this one sloping steeply to the stream. To prevent the brook's burrowing and grinding forces from undermining the land, the owners, a long time ago, laid up rocks against the bank. In some places the retaining wall reaches four feet above today's water level. I forget that this tranquil summer flow would be unrecognizable at other times. Torrents flung against the banks in spring or in response to deluges carry away the land. Big stones curb a brook's unbridled enthusiasm, at least for a time.

Near the base of the retaining wall, Parmenter drops steeply into a pool, which appears to be child-made. A line of medium-sized rocks crosses the brook. Sticks and debris, caught by the rocks, impound Parmenter's water in a three-foot deep, three-yard wide pool. The rocks creating the dam are laid out in a single line—intriguing but not serious engineering. I suspect this was a summer project, an attempt to make a fishing hole or a place for small people to splash. I think the work is not more than a few years old, much too recent for me or my cousins to have had a hand in it. It pleases me to think some youngster since my time busied himself or herself investigating Parmenter's dynamism.

The flowing water and I approach the fourth stone wall in our course. Like the walls upstream, this one too has tumbled into the brook bed. But this remnant bears a distinctive feature. Stakes carrying broken strands of barbed wire protrude from the spaces between the big rocks. This is not only a wall, it is a fence, or it once was a fence. Now I recognize where I have come. This ruined artifact in Parmenter's way is special. These are strands of barbed wire my father and I stretched and stapled. They replaced fencing erected by his father before him and very likely by George Parmenter before that. Parmenter Brook has at last reached its namesake homestead and flows onto my family's land from Bass Farm.

Eben Bass and George Parmenter were longtime neighbors, as John Whiton and Amos had been before them. George worked for Eben off and on for a number of years. In May, 1877, Eben hired George and his team of oxen three days in a row for $8.25. George's daybook doesn't specify what the long job was. I like to think that the manpower and oxpower were applied building or repairing a stone wall, perhaps this very one.

Downstream of the old fence, where our pasture ran to the banks of Parmenter Brook, I'm happy to find a small flock of sheep, six white and a black, watching me. They are penned inside some electrified fencing in Amos Parmenter's North Field, and watered through a hose from a well at a house nearby. They cannot come where I am to drink from the stream or rest in the shade of the middle-aged pines and poplars that grow on the brook bank. Even if they were not fenced, they would be severely challenged to find a way to Parmenter's water, so tight together are the alder trunks and so thick the unbroken hedge of prickly blackberry canes and wild rose stems.

As I approach NH Route 31 running along the east border of the pasture, Parmenter is noisy, as it falls over large stones in its streambed. Where it makes a sharp bend along the pasture margin I discover what appears to be a broad pavement of stones, as if the pasture rim had been cobbled once upon a time. Perhaps this is only a collapsed and buried rock pile, but I think the stones may have been carefully laid down like pavers to prevent the pasture edge from being worn away by Parmenter's spring thrust. I take it as evidence of a man's determined effort to hold back his land from a run to the sea.

The stonework I've seen testifies to the dynamism of Parmenter Brook. It may be little more than an "unpretending rill" today (to borrow from Wordsworth), slowed by thirsty brush and weeds thick along its edges, but the will of the water could not always be ignored. The water gate at Lily Pond, the rock overpass lost in the woods, the retaining wall, and now the cobbling at a pasture's edge—each tell me that Parmenter Brook was taken into consideration, was attended to, when men made a living off this land. I confess that I can't get enough of the story Parmenter tells.

12

When Amos Parmenter settled his family here, the "leading road" connecting the Contoocook River, which borders one edge of the township to Antrim Center a few miles north, did not pass by his farm, but soon after he arrived, laid down in sections, a new and straighter road to the Center cut his farm in two and ran over his brook on a stone overpass. Did Amos consider the new road a boon to his business or a major inconvenience to his farming chores? It's hard to know, except that a few years after the new road appeared, he built an impressive brick house across the new highway from his cabin site but left his barns on the side where his cabin stood. Going back and forth across the road from his new house to his old barns must not have seemed such a great nuisance. The busy barns were not moved to stand beside the new house for another fifty years.

I am about to cross the road that divided Amos's farm, now a paved street with heavy traffic, to follow Parmenter Brook as it falls out of a culvert into the fire hole.

Fire hole. Not for building a fire, but for impounding water to use in case of fire. There is no record of the history of the Clinton fire hole, but when the beautiful home Amos Parmenter built in 1827 burned to the ground seventy years later, the destruction was not attributed to a shortage of water, but rather to poor roads impeding fire fighting apparatus, so perhaps the fire hole, some four hundred feet from his house, was already established. I knew the fire hole as swimming pool, fishing site, skating rink and a boy's hydro engineering laboratory. It was never called on to fulfill its intended purpose while I was around.

My playmates were my cousins, descended, like me, from one of George Parmenter's daughters. The boys lived next door to the farm, and when their parents or mine were looking for us they began at the fire hole. Maybe because this quasi-municipal facility received only sporadic attention by the fire department, my cousins and I assumed the role of overseers. As we grew older and stronger, our management of the fire hole became more vigorous. We cut the weeds that grew around it so that we could swim in the sun. We lifted out rocks to add depth for cannonballing from the road edge. We added flashboards to the dam so that we could control the flow. In peak condition, the fire hole contained water four or five feet deep in a pool several yards across, deepest where Parmenter dropped out of the culvert, shallower at the silted dam end.

The culvert was itself a source of hot-day entertainment. Crawling upstream through its cold, slimy concrete darkness (concrete replaced stonework early in the twentieth century), especially when we knew a gravel truck bearing a full load was about to pass just inches above our heads, we considered a wildly courageous thing to do. As we crept through the chilly ooze, we heightened the excitement by imagining that the road might collapse and trap us there, or that the beaver dam at Lily Pond might give way and we would be drowned in the rushing flood. That we might actually somehow be crushed or drowned was not part of our reality, it was all just pretend.

Death in general, though, was familiar to my cousins and me. No one growing up on a farm is unacquainted with death. Though it's a sad mystery, we knew that sometimes it's a blessing. No animal on the farm should be allowed to suffer. The farm boy learns that early. His own thoughtlessness is quickly corrected, and he sees the lengths to which his father will go to relieve the apparent pain of an injured animal or the misery of being surplus. Life and death and suffering were running jumbled in our heads the day cousin Kenny and I contemplated a weighty challenge.

Cats are at the top of a short food chain on a farm. Grain, however securely stored, must be measured out and strewn in the open for cows, pigs and chickens to consume. Loose grain attracts mice and rats. Cats, in turn, feed on rodents. With few natural enemies in or around the barn, cat populations soar at times, bringing disease and defilement. It was for the good of all, Kenny and I were told, that the latest litter should be sacrificed. Drowning, we were led to understand, was a humane method of mass extermination.

Confident that we could carry out the miserable task, we gathered the five kittens, and one by one forced them against their natural, scratching resistance into a burlap grain bag. We carefully added a few ballast stones, and tied the bag shut. Taking turns carrying the heavy, squirming, mewing load to the fire hole, our confidence waned, for neither of us wanted to be the last one to hold the bag over the deep water.

After what seemed to us sufficient time for the kittens to breathe their last, we retrieved the quiet bag. We opened it to remove the heavy stones and out crept the dazed kittens. Grain dust between the threads of burlap, I now reason, must have swelled in the water and sealed the cats in a bubble of air. It was simply the kittens' lucky day as far as Kenny and I were concerned. No one asked questions, and we volunteered nothing.

The Clinton fire hole is silted to ineffective shallowness, its dam washed away, and its basin crowded to little more than a puddle by weeds, brush and saplings. I can almost straddle the place where Parmenter Brook pooled to feed a boy's creativity.

Barges come to mind. Fashioned from pieces of scrap lumber I could always find in my father's workshop, these brightly painted, rubber band-propelled vessels made for off-and-on entertainment for my cousins and me. With a keyhole saw we cut a notch into one end of a ten-to-twelve-inch board. A strong rubber band, like the kind that the mailman used to attach packages to our mailboxes, flipped a paddle wound up in this stern notch. A pointed bow cut by hand (never mind that a barge has no prow) seemed to make our boats cut through water more easily. We raced the barges against and with the fire hole's weak current. We loaded them with stones, twigs, or piles of sand to test their power. A small turtle seemed not to mind a free ride. The most challenging cargo to lade and carry was a live frog. Some days our painted-board regatta drew a small audience. A green frog sitting like a prince on a red barge was a crowd pleaser.

13

Leaving the cheers and jeers behind, I pick up Parmenter where it exits the fire hole. It is early morning, a bright day, and the shadow falling over me, literally and figuratively, is cast by a large house and barn atop a steep road cut that runs beside the brook. The bank supporting the looming buildings is littered with singed and broken bricks. The buildings that are casting shade over Parmenter Brook replaced Amos Parmenter's brick house in 1897.

My great-grandfather Bill Butterfield and his son Charles worked together to erect the wood-frame, federal-style farmhouse where my father, his siblings, and my sister and I grew up. Bill had married George Parmenter's daughter Abbie when he returned from duty in Washington, DC, at the end of the Civil War, and my grandfather, for whom I am named, was the second of their eight children. Though they began their married life and reared their children in Antrim Center, when her father died, Abbie and Bill borrowed money to buy the Parmenter place in Clinton from her mother and other heirs. And then, before her family moved the half-mile to the homestead, Abbie died of poison by her own hand. For some time, she had suffered from a stomach ailment, and with the diagnosis of cancer, she could take no more, and, we are told, swallowed iodine.

SEEKING PARMENTER

Bill Butterfield, inheriting his wife's debt and large property, turned to his oldest son, then twenty-four years old and just married, for help. Charles's young family and Bill's teenagers moved to the Parmenter place to care for Abbie's aged and blind mother. Father and son established a poultry business. But four years into their enterprise, the brick house Amos Parmenter had built for his second wife burned to the ground one October morning.

The replacement house, set on the old foundation, took shape quickly, the burned and broken bricks shoved over the bank behind the house. Amos Parmenter's barn was moved from across the road and connected to the new house by a two-story woodshed in typical New England linked architecture. Uninterrupted by the fire, the hen business flourished. When my sister and I emptied the house attic many years later, we found dozens of medallions and ribbons awarded to Butterfield chickens in poultry competitions around the state. With chickens, the Parmenter place morphed into Butterfield Farm.

I move with the brook below and behind the farmhouse and barn and into full sunshine. Between the barn and the stone culvert where my grandmother and I sailed fern boats under the road, I come upon a pleasant surprise.

Old photos of many houses in Antrim, including the Butterfield house, feature American elms gracing dooryards. Once immensely favored for their elegant, fountain-shaped crown, elms died out in the 1950s and '60s, their internal transport systems plugged by a fungus carried by bark beetles. Only a few of the magnificent trees survive. One beautiful, rare specimen stands in Antrim Center next to the first town hall where Amos Parmenter moderated town meetings. But streets and dooryards are mostly vacant now of elms. While saplings do grow out of old rootstock, most die when they are attacked by infected bark beetles.

So I'm surprised to find a sizable clump of American elms standing twenty feet tall, lush and green in the morning sun. I count five trees with diameters between sixteen and twenty inches. These are mature trees. Fissures are beginning to form in the bark. It is these fissures that invite the two bark beetles that carry Dutch elm disease. In a few years I will know for sure whether or not these trees are resistant to the dreaded *Ceratocystis ulmi*. For now, this stand brings hope that Butterfield Farm may once again be shaded and cooled as I remember.

Downstream of the clustered elms, Parmenter meanders through a former pasture/orchard where my great-grandfather's apples still grow and where my father's milk cows grazed. Barberry and sumac stand thick on the sloping terrain, and as I force my way through, I rather hope the luxuriant overgrowth slows runoff into the brook, because the otherwise pristine stream has been compromised for many years by two features on this part of the farm.

Hidden in the apple trees and out of sight of the house and barn, our family's dump received all manner of household and barn trash—discarded tools, dishes, leaky pots and pans, worn-out pails and tubs, chicken wire, tires, broken barrels, paint cans, mattresses, pillows, abandoned furniture and useless pieces of lumber. My cousins and I developed our pitching arms at the dump, aiming rocks at glass bottles and jars set up as targets. At the dump I discovered balls of real tinfoil (not aluminum foil) the size of baseballs that I kept as treasures for years. A coarse, white powder, never identified, maybe a chicken remedy, melted in the rain and joined generations of pollutant stew leaching into the soil under the dump and seeping into Parmenter.

Between the dump and the brook, on a level stretch, we buried the farm dead. The ground received carcasses of sheep, cows, horses, cats and beloved dogs. Their degraded proteins are probably still slowly making their way through the soil into Parmenter Brook along with oxidized metal and petroleum products leaking from abandoned chassis dragged there to rust out of sight.

Just beyond the graveyard, the brook flows through the fifth and final stone wall positioned along its course. Because this wall was, until some sixty years ago, a cattle fence as well as a property bound, we looked after it. The split chestnut fence posts carrying strands of barbed wire remain. We replaced frost-spilled stones, and shored up those subject to the brook's undermining action, though the nearly level land on which the wall stands aided us in that. Here there is no crashing tumult of water in flood season. When there is an excess of water, it simply flows out across the flat terrain and waits on the surface until the stream can accommodate it.

Here, finally, his namesake brook flows away from what remains of Amos Parmenter's farm that has never passed entirely out of the hands of those he seeded.

Gary Snyder quotes a Crow elder: "You know, I think if people stay somewhere long enough—even white people—the spirits will begin to speak to them. It's the power of the spirits coming up from the land. The spirits and the old powers aren't lost, they just need people to be around long enough and the spirits will begin to influence them."

I'm disinclined to think "spirits," but this walk down Parmenter Brook certainly does tie me closely to those I am heir to. For a few minutes, I poke around the final yards of Parmenter acreage looking for some piece of trash I might remember throwing away in this corner of the farm. I find a large decayed bone, bleached white and moss covered, one end gnawed. I believe it's the femur of an ox (too bulky for a cow, too stubby for a horse). Was a worn-out ox once buried here and this piece unearthed the way rocks are heaved up by frost action? As far as I know, the last farmer to work oxen on this place was George Parmenter a hundred fifty years ago. I know that the subsequent Butterfields relied on horses for power before there were tractors. Is this bone old enough to have belonged to one of my great-great-grandfather's animals? There is no way for me to know, and possibly this bone was dragged here from some other place by a carnivore since George's time, but my long, intimate walk from Lily Pond to the edge of his farm where I remember digging animal graves makes me want to believe that I'm holding the skeleton of a flank George Parmenter once currycombed and brushed.

14

From Lily Pond to the spot where I step over this final stone wall, Parmenter Brook has dropped about 200 feet in just over three-fourths of a mile. If the drop occurred in a much shorter distance, say an eighth of a mile, the water would have enough force to turn a waterwheel. But stretched out as it is, the flow develops no serious power, and no mill ever sat beside Parmenter.

But from this wall to its confluence with Great Brook, Parmenter drops 130 feet in elevation in a little less than half a mile, and most of that in about three-tenths of a mile. In other words, the water in Parmenter Brook falls with determination near its terminus. This feature might well have provided some interest in putting in a millrace. Only one thing discouraged such an idea. Great Brook, where Parmenter is heading, is a much larger stream falling much faster.

The power in Great Brook was transferred to as many as half a dozen mill wheels in Clinton Village. That busy settlement turned its back on Parmenter Brook. Literally. From my perch at the top of Parmenter's final descent—a respectable, noisy slosh among huge boulders—I look west and see only the backs of houses and a large storage barn that was once the property of the Abbott Company, manufacturer of caskets, cribs, cradles and playpens, the screams of its saws and planers and sanders translating the power in Great Brook.

Though the mill whistles and machinery are silenced, I hear the harsh clatter of diesel engines, the rattle of bulldozers, and catch a glimpse of dump trucks hauling material from one place to another in the gravel works atop the high bank above Parmenter Brook. Black plastic sheeting staked several feet back from the water's edge protects the brook from silting by erosion of mountains of earth. It occurs to me that the same glacial grinding that carved out this deep ravine fifteen thousand years ago deposited the layers of gravel now being dug up and hauled away to construction sites. The roar of the belching engines I hear is but a whisper compared to the thunderous explosions of shattering bedrock and the air-riving screeches of boulders being torn to bits under tons of ice long, long ago.

In following this brook through the farms it has watered, I learned this: a natural symbiosis develops between the land and those who farm it. Amos Parmenter cleared off trees and turned his virgin soil in order to make this land productive as he defined productivity. But he worked within constraints. His New Hampshire climate, his rock-ribbed terrain, and the ingredients that thousands of years of native plant decomposition had worked into his soil dictated what crops he could grow. They worked together, land and settler.

I am in thrall to the idea that once upon a time this was a wild place, sufficient unto itself, and through generations of those who drew their living from it, it was tamed and became intimately incorporated into their lives. They made the land what it became; the land made them what they became. An extraordinary mutualism developed that I am privileged to have shared. It is as if the Parmenters and the Butterfields are urging me to negotiate with the land and climate. Restrain yourself, they say to me, for the good of the ecosystem you are a part of. Take yourself off any pedestal your culture may have devised for you and be at home on the ground in this place.

At Parmenter's terminus I give in to a strong impulse to celebrate. Stooping, I collect some dry hemlock twigs and weave them together, fashioning a tiny raft. I make a garland of birch leaves and place it on the woven deck and set it afloat in Parmenter. I watch as it drifts, at first leisurely, even reluctantly, then picks up speed as it is tugged into the meeting with Great

SEEKING PARMENTER

Brook. The frail vessel tilts and bobs in the stronger rush before it floats around the bend, hugging the outside bank, and with Parmenter, heads to the sea.

IV
Parmenter Without Us

*Whatever attitude to human existence you fashion for yourself,
know that it is valid only if it be the shadow of an attitude to Nature.*

HENRY BESTON

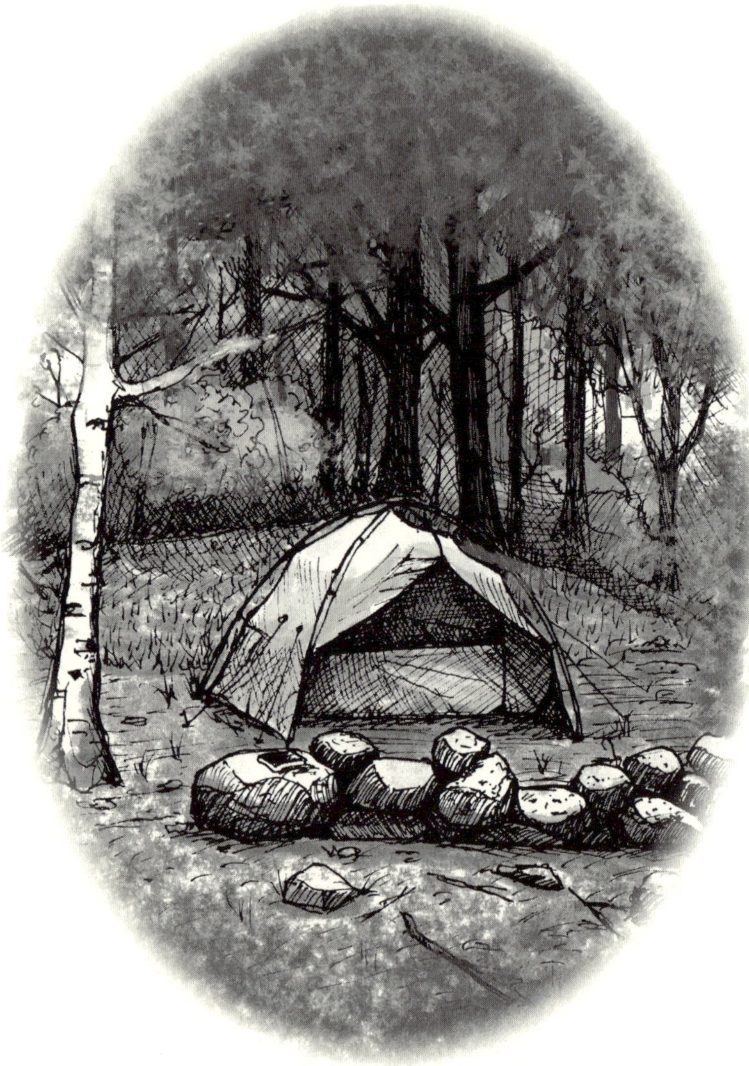

Caucus-Meteor, the appealing protagonist in Ernest Hebert's novel *The Old American*, is the dubious chief of a nomadic group of Native Americans with visions of himself as King of America. Such high ambition raises doubts about his true place in the world; long nights he contemplates his destiny, peering into burning sticks, "eating his fire."

This ordinary evening, sitting before my own fire, I read a little and write notes by the light of an LED lamp strapped to my forehead. Tiring of that, I turn on my solar-powered radio and catch a few innings of Red Sox baseball before the battery runs out of charge. But mostly I eat my fire and think about Parmenter without us.

I can't conjure as Caucus-Meteor does and thus control events, but I can contemplate. There are plenty of imponderables to keep me occupied as pine smoke burns my eyes. For instance, what will become of the Parmenter place? The decision is not mine to make. I saw to that when I deeded the last piece of the old farm to nieces and nephews. Even so, I cannot help but consider the changes that may come to this place in the next ten or fifty years.

What do I wish might become of it? My first choice is that it be protected by a conservation easement so that no developer can come along and bulldoze house lots here. That's a selfish and expensive option. It would suit me because I could continue to clamber over these rocky acres and observe the next few stages of wildness coming on.

The idea gains strength in my mind from the fact that in my rambles I've discovered that this small acreage now abuts extensive protected tracts on the north and west. Still, because this land has been home to eight generations of my family, deep down I have the feeling that it should continue to serve my or another family for years to come. Thus I eat my fire, pondering Parmenter land, peopled or wild.

Tonight, there is abundant wildness around me, wildness with its own concerns. Though I can't see them, bats, chipmunks, possibly porcupines, notice my firelight through the trees and doubtless consider, in their own way, what it means for them. Some insects fly into my flames, others shun my smoke and the fire's aroma. And, as Daniel Chamovitz so expertly explains in *What a Plant Knows*, the trees and weeds I can barely make out in the dark are sort of aware of what is going on.

Chamovitz tells me that while the trees don't know me specifically, and are not paying attention to my sitting here, they are capable of detecting my smoke, and my flames emit photons they respond to. Perhaps the pines woodenly shudder when my sparks fly through their needles. When I sawed off limbs to burn, the tree knew it and started to seal the wound. When I dug this fire pit with my folding shovel, the roots I tore to pieces detected the damage and reacted to repair it, even signaling the disturbance to the roots of adjoining plants. Chamovitz recounts dozens of experiments carried out by plant physiologists in pursuit of knowledge about plant sensitivity, and learning about what they have found out causes me to ponder the depth of this forest's awareness of my presence as I eat my fire.

SEEKING PARMENTER

Since Charles Darwin experimented with seedlings, we've known that plants sense their environment. Amos Parmenter, working mostly in ignorance of soil chemistry, knew well enough that there was something in Lily Pond peat that his potatoes cried out for. George Parmenter, just a year younger than Darwin, watched his oat and barley seedlings twist and bend to catch the best light. My great-grandfather's apple trees knew where their water was and reached for it. My father's ladino clover, its white-flowered stems creeping across his pasture, responded to his scientifically-conditioned soil.

These days it is pines, hemlocks, white ash, red oaks, gray birch and black cherry that talk among themselves about soil conditions, acid rain and insect damage. Can hemlocks adapt to the invading woolly adelgid? Can ash trees evolve protective mechanisms under the pressure of invading emerald bark beetles? The mature elms behind the barn—have they successfully resisted the bark beetles that felled their mighty ancestors that I watched nudge root pads as they swayed in the furious winds of the '38 hurricane? What protective mechanisms can the trees in these woods employ in the presence of new foes? Will enemies of tree enemies released by foresters be my friends? One old man enveloped in pine smoke wants to know.

I have wandered for days where this forest emerges slowly from foraged fields, an inevitable transformation given the limits to growth on a small, family farm. I recall my father trying to help me understand a basic principle of capitalism, namely that there must be expansion and the expectation of expansion if a business enterprise is to prosper. A company that isn't growing is dying, he said. I wish I could remember the context of his remarks. Perhaps some local shop we both knew had just laid off workers. But perhaps, regardless of the immediate circumstances, he was preparing me for the changes that would come to our farm someday.

He understood that in the Parmenter era, it took only a little growth to assure success from year to year. He knew also that growing markets and competition made possible by improved transportation like the Erie Canal and later the railroad meant that prosperity depended on more and more production. Though Amos had acquired several hundred acres for pasture and crops, land by itself was not enough to sustain his descendants. New enterprises boosted economic viability for a time—beef cattle gave way to orchards, orchards to chickens, chickens to dairy cows. But in the end, I think my father was telling me, our small-farm capitalism could fail. And so it did, abetted, in his personal situation, by advancing age and declining health.

My free-ranging reverie is interrupted by sounds on the night air I mostly ignore by day. Far off a dog's barking sounds cautionary in the dark. A dead branch snaps, a wing flutters, dry leaves rustle and questions arise. Is something I can't see coming toward me? I'm not afraid of the night forest, and I want to pay attention, to wait and watch, but I'm fatigued from this day's hiking, and I doze in front of my fire. My wood burns down, and my dimming senses cut me off from the forest's business.

I douse the embers, stash my gear under the awnings of the tent, though there's no hint of rain, and zip myself within the fabric screens without closing the weather flaps. Stretched out on my cot, I draw my sleeping bag around me and for a few minutes attend to the voices of trees.

2

In his best-selling book, *The World Without Us*, Alan Weisman describes how the world would change if human beings suddenly and completely disappeared. He tells what would become of our cities and their connecting interstates, our nuclear plants and their stored waste, our farms and domesticated animals and plants, our monuments and ancient temples, and everything else we have made. Weisman's ambitious thought experiment asks: "How would the rest of nature respond if it were suddenly relieved of the relentless pressures we heap on it?"

This old farm, its brook and its stone walls, is not yet bereft of, or blessed by, the total absence of humans, of course. But in the years since Butterfield Farm ceased operations in the mid-twentieth century, this place has been increasingly relieved of the relentless pressure generations of my family heaped on it. Now, as I write about them, the remaining thirty-three acres are for sale. Regardless of their fate, the life forms these acres support will continue to respond to the effects of human air pollution. The interval between the soil's spring thawing and winter freezing will continue to lengthen, a consequence of anthropogenic global warming. In the wake of this warming creep, insects and other wildlife and plants unfamiliar to me will settle into niches here. Transformation is nothing new to the old Parmenter-Butterfield place; still I wonder . . .

Does Parmenter Brook miss us? Does it care that no cow dung adds fragrance and taste to its water, or that lime and phosphate are no longer running off the slanted fields into its stream? Does it miss children splashing in its water and roiling its silted bed? Is it bothered that budding anglers find no fish or frogs in habitats it once provided? Our touch is lighter now, our requirements of it almost nonexistent. As ours was but a temporary influence, perhaps the brook is looking and feeling more like its old self.

Does the long wall yearn for its spring repairs? Where a rock has tumbled off, does the wall wait for strong arms to lift it back in place? When blackflies swarm does it anticipate the appearance of man and boy with wire and freshly cut posts to mend the fence? I like to think the stones in the wall recall their slow exposure from under thick ice and then the eons that they lay buried under thick earth until Amos rudely awakened them as he slashed and burned and carried away their forest cover. Perhaps the stones remember the time before Amos disrupted everything over and around them, and feel a time of long sleeping settling over them again.

I wonder.

3

I left the farm in the winter of 1955, a few months after I graduated from college. An Air Force ROTC second lieutenant, I was obliged to fulfill my military stint, and I chose to leave wintry Antrim in February for training in the medical service corps in sunny Montgomery, Alabama. I made a good choice. The training matched my biology major, and I put to use the anatomy and physiology I'd learned. I flourished in the classroom, and I didn't flub up seriously on the drill field or firing range.

To boot, a Yankee boy learned something about Jim Crow.

SEEKING PARMENTER

On a trip into the city, in uniform, I offered my seat on an overcrowded bus to an African-American woman. She was tired, but she couldn't accept my offer because my seat was in front of the white line painted on the floor. By law she could stand there, but she couldn't sit down, and she allowed as much. So we both stood in the aisle until she left the bus. I think now that the Yankee boy made a mistake since neither of us gained anything, and he only called attention to her plight, but at the time his refusal to sit as long as she was required to stand felt like the right thing to do. Six months later Rosa Parks was arrested for refusing to give up her seat on a Montgomery bus to a white man.

Training done, I was assigned to a small hospital at an Air Force base in Washington, DC. I assisted the adjutant of the hospital squadron from eight to five, and attended George Washington University in the evening to pursue a master's degree in education. When the military obligation was discharged, I attended school full time until I landed a job as biology teacher in a posh Washington suburb the same year that the USSR launched *Sputnik*. That event opened US faucets for funding science and math education, and our kids and their teachers began to catch up to the Soviets in technology. It was exactly the right time for me to begin my thirty-eight-year science-teaching career.

In the meantime, Butterfield Farm ceased operations, and in time my sister and I inherited the sixty or so acres that remained of the old Parmenter place. Neither of us had an interest in farming, so the buildings were rented and the fields and forests sprouted second growth. We gave parcels of land to her children, sold some small sections to neighbors, and in a convoluted manner the house Bill Butterfield built on Amos Parmenter's burned-out foundation passed to one of Amos's great-great-great-great granddaughters.

Late in retirement, I began these long camping sojourns on land where first I played and later farmed. My tent site beside the old orchard may soon pass into a stranger's hands, and my connection with this place will, in one sense, come to an end. In another sense, I cannot be separated from what is a permanent part of my inner landscape.

4

When I speak of my summer sojourns at this grown-over farm, people reply, "Oh, getting back to nature, eh?" But when are we ever not in nature? When Amos cleared land along its brook and planted barley where primeval pines formerly grew, and measured off and walled his pastures with rocks, was that not natural? Was the brook in any sense less natural when it flowed through fodder than when it ran through forest? Are rocks less in a state of nature when they are lined up or piled than when they lie scattered?

"Nature is everything, OK?" writes essayist and critic Hayden Carruth, "not merely stones and oceans, butterflies and flowers, but ideas, poems, dreams, spiritual intimations." So nature is, among other things, an idea, a concept, and like other mental constructs it has changed over time. The concept of nature that we need today is one that includes the interaction and interdependence of human and nonhuman elements of our environment. We need to scrap the idea that there was once a more perfect world, and that we can return to some version of it if we just cut back on our energy consumption, curb our population growth, and eat only locally grown, organic food. As necessary to our continued existence as steps like these may be, they do not lead to a reassessment of the basic relationship humans have with the rest of the planet. We cannot continue to think and act on the premise that a boundary exists between nature and society.

To think of ourselves and our activities as separate from and alien to nature is to create a fictional, and I believe dangerous, dichotomy. Picturing human society as something separate from nature leads, on the one hand, to a reckless disregard for what some choose to call "not us." Nature, we may suppose, is there to be exploited with abandon so that human society can flourish. Amos Parmenter may have believed that, but his descendants know folly that way lies.

On the other hand, acting as if there are two distinct and separate states of existence can promote a protective idealization of anything that isn't human or of human origin. To think of nature as some wild state from which humans are, or should be, excluded, is to ignore the reality that humans already influence, directly and indirectly, every nook and cranny of the world. The extent of human effect varies from place to place on the globe, but we insinuate ourselves everywhere. What is more, our impact is part and parcel of nature.

There are those who say to me, "But surely you don't consider a city slum with nightly murders and drug-related mayhem natural. Surely a river so polluted with hydrocarbons that it catches fire is not natural. CFCs destroying the protective ozone layer cannot be a natural phenomenon." To all of which I reply, human beings brought about these calamitous conditions out of ignorance or denial of natural laws. They can be managed, though not until human beings employ the natural law of consequences to change the causes. It is because we forgot, or never understood, how much we are always in a state of nature that these and many other deplorable and destructive situations arose and are arising. Because we thought we were separate from nature, maybe better than nature, we believed we had nothing to fear from the consequences of our presumed independence. We forgot, or failed to understand, that there is no independence *from* nature, only interdependence *with* nature.

If I say good-bye to a visitor who has dropped by my tent to chat and then I leave the woods to walk alone up the highway past my old school, being careful to stay out of the lanes of traffic, squeeze through a fence and scramble among tall weeds taking over an abandoned sheep pasture, step across the brook, enter the long-undisturbed woods, and finally climb a steep, pathless ledge still bearing glacier marks to where I can look down on Lily Pond a hundred feet below, where along that route did I cross a line and enter nature? And was that isolated overlook in a state of nature before I arrived, only to slip out of it when I showed up?

It seems to me that were we to replace the idea of a society/nature divide with the idea of a society–nature integration, we would be better equipped to take up the environmental problems we are coping with. Maybe if each of us adopted some little piece of the planet and allowed a sense of kinship to develop between the self and that chosen place, we would begin to appreciate that there is no line dividing human from nature. As Chet Raymo says, "When you know one place well—not just intellectually but with the deep-gut knowledge that enters through the soles of your feet—connections just keep popping up." It is connections we need, not separation.

Not long ago I sat with a small group of tree huggers talking about what initially caused them to care about our environment. Several in the group told of a favorite childhood experience in the woods, on the banks of a brook, or the shores of a lake, that stayed with them into their adult lives. It seemed to them that it was a positive encounter with something in that scene early on that awakened them to the relationship they wanted to have with Earth. For them, one touch of wildness grew into an affinity with the interdependent web of life.

This strikes me as a strong argument for providing children the opportunity to know some little place in the out-of-doors. A child may grow a kinship with that place and choose to become its custodian. From such little beginnings, kinship may spread to the fish in the sea, the birds of the air, the minerals under the soil, even the infrastructure we build and depend on.

And my advice to the grey heads I know so well: touch wildness. Find some place where the walking is safe, the sounds inhuman, the smells easy on the nose, and where earth tones dominate the scene. Stay there long enough for some deep-gut knowledge to enter the soles of your feet. Oh, I know a walk in the woods or along the shore is impossible for the infirm. But touching the wild through an open window can suffice, even a car window. The point is to touch the wild in a manner that can induce kinship with place.

By now it must be clear that where the Parmenter family lived and worked for generations played that role in my life. I experienced it early and it has spoken to me ever since. It might seem that I would regret its current disheveled and weed-blocked condition. But no, as I see and feel it, it is a gift to the Parmenter place to let it grow young and wild again.

This morning, after breaking camp for the season, I walked to the swampy brook edge. As I approached the crowded ferns, elderberry bushes and bright yellow St. Johnswort, tasting the mixed aromas in the warm air, a red-winged blackbird dive-bombed my head. In his opinion I was getting dangerously close to his family's territory. I stepped away, and it came to me that the brook edge, messy with overlapping habitats, is highly attractive in the eyes of some wildlife, and that if I reserve judgment drawn from my history on this land, and think strictly about biomass and diversity, the banks of Parmenter Brook are every bit as functional today as when they were grazed and tamped by the cows I drove to their milking.

The brook and the stone wall remind me that out of one ecosystem another emerges. Prior to Amos Parmenter's arrival in Antrim, there was the ecology of primeval forest here, maybe slightly modified by Native Americans. During the Parmenter-Butterfield era the ecology was very much the domain of industrious farmers. Today, what's left of Amos Parmenter's farm ecologists call, sensibly enough, "old field." Each ecosystem, with or without my family, was and is a natural state.

5

"Grandsir' met me at the depot as usual. As I looked from the car window I saw him standing on the platform at the station, waiting. What a fine looking old gentleman he was! Tall and

well-built—beautiful, silvery white hair and keen black eyes. He was always happy and it was a rest to look at his pleasant face."

Evie Butterfield, my grandfather's older sister, is describing her grandfather, George Parmenter, as she remembered him on an occasion some five months before the old man died in 1890.

It was a rest. Nice phrase, that. I take it to mean a combination of quiet comfort and peaceful encouragement. Evie's Grandsir' was known for miles around for the gift of healing that his Scots-Irish Presbyterian acquaintances attributed to him as a seventh-son doctor. From at least the sixteenth century, some people of Celtic descent held to the notion that a seventh-born son, with no intervening sisters, could cure various illnesses by the application of a talisman. (My grandmother told me that George placed a small pendant around a patient's neck.) For Evie, apparently, looking on the old man's bearded face alone was curative.

It was a rest. I have walked to many places on and around the old Parmenter place where Evie's phrase applies. Parmenter Brook flows over moss-carpeted granite tiers without a sound. That's a rest. A section of stone wall climbs up a hill, catching the sun in its many angled facets. That's a rest. The old road, needle carpeted, stretches out between its parallel granite bounds in a summer rain. That's a rest. A lichen-covered boulder warmed in the sun gives off a subtly metallic aroma. That's a rest. My blue tent, light-dappled, and viewed through an avenue of white pines. That's a rest.

I've studied the structural complexity of old-field ecological succession. I've tried to figure out the logic of stone wall construction and placement. I've been drawn to the artifacts of an agrarian culture and to the enduring evidence of a settlement's once flourishing businesses. I've visited gravestones and monuments erected "in memory of." In short, I've gone back to former times and found it a rest.

I've also visited new houses in erstwhile hay fields and beside old millponds. I've seen how Parmenter Brook has been tamed to accommodate new roads. I've measured big pines, ready for harvesting, standing tall above stumps dating from previous harvests. I've watched that slim, young woman plant ornamental grasses and perennials, beautifying an ancient stone wall. In the quiet of a former mowing, I've looked around me at the baffling array of forbs and shrubs and saplings springing up where once a farmer cultivated only a few chosen grains. Everywhere there are signs of growth, diversity and emergence, and that's a rest.

Appendixes

George Parmenter's Obligation

Note: Bolded portions are text of the printed form, the rest is handwritten in the original, presumably by John F. Brown, Concord, NH, who prepared and sold this document to the Parmenters.

Know all men by these presents that *I, George F. Parmenter of Antrim in County of Hillsborough and State of New Hampshire am* **held and firmly bound** *to Amos Parmenter of Town, County and State aforesaid* **in the sum** *of two thousand dollars* **to be paid to the said** *Amos Parmenter* **or** *his* **heirs, certain attorney, executors, administrators or assigns, to which payment well and truly to be made** *I* **bind** *myself and my* **heirs, executors and administrators firmly by these Presents. Sealed with** *my* **seal and dated the** *sixth* **day of** *March* **A.D. 1848.**

The condition of this Obligation is such, that if the above bound *George F. Parmenter,* **his heirs, executors or administrators do and shall well and truly** *carry on the farm this day deeded by A. Parmenter to G. F. Parmenter in a seasonable and workmanlike manner and shall every year during the natural life of the said Amos Parmenter deliver to him, the said A. Parmenter, one half of all the income of said farm, and at his decease (if she shall outlive him) shall deliver to Hannah wife of the said A. Parmenter one fourth of all the income of said farm, that is to say one half of the grain, potatoes, apples and other vegetable productions of the farm, one half of the produce of the dairy, the work of carrying on the dairy to be done by G. F. Parmenter which dairy shall always consist of four cows or more, one half of the beef and pork and half the income* of the poultry and one half the income of the stock which is to be owned in common, the hay to be spent on the farm and if any of it is ever sold one half the proceeds to go to the said A. Parmenter, and shall at all times keep a steady and suitable horse for the use of the said A. Parmenter and his wife and if the horse so kept for their use shall not be safe for them to use he, the said G. F. Parmenter, shall himself go and carry the said A. Parmenter and his wife wherever their request is proper and reasonable, and if the oxen shall at any time do any more work than what is required in doing the oxwork of the farm, one half the income of said labor shall go to A. Parmenter, and shall keep the farming tools in suitable repair at his own expense and shall at all times give and grant to the said Parmenter and his wife the free use and occupation of the room in which they now live, it being the west room in the old part of the house, the chamber over the same, the south room in the new part of the house with the chamber over it, the front entry leading west, with a privilege of using the stairs in the same, the west cellar, the back room north of the room first named except a privilege of passing though the northeast back room to the shed, the entry in the old part of the house together with the right of occupying the shed, out buildings and barn for all necessary purposes whatever, and the front yard west of the house, and shall pay one half of the taxes on the farm and on the stock owned in common and shall seasonably deliver to the said A. Parmenter in their proper and usual places his share of the productions of the farm and all other articles, and shall at all times furnish a good and sufficient supply of firewood cut and prepared fit for a stove or fireplace, one half at least of which shall be dry and all to be put in the shed in good order and shall always at the expense of the G. F. Parmenter procure and furnish for the said A. Parmenter and Hannah his wife all necessary help and attendance in sickness and at all times suitable and seasonable medical attendance and medicine and shall do and perform all those offices which are required to make old age comfortable, and if the said Hannah outlives the said A. Parmenter and should choose to live on her right of dower in the premises, then the said G. F. Parmenter is to be released from carrying in said fourth part of the income to the said Hannah Parmenter, and the conditions *and agreements of this Bond are to be fulfilled and performed in the buildings on the farm where they, the said A. and G. F. Parmenter now live, and in no other place unless it is agreed on by the parties concerned.*

Then this obligation to be void, otherwise to be and remain in full force and virtue.

/s/ *George F. Parmenter*

Signed, sealed and delivered in presence of

/s/ *E. L. Vose*
/s/ *Aurelia Vose*
Sold by John F. Brown, Concord, N.H.

The Generations

First

Amos Parmenter and wife Tryphena Bannister came to Antrim with two-year-old Nancy in 1800. The couple raised eight sons and three daughters. Amos, a devout churchman, established the Central Society Meetinghouse (Presbyterian affiliation) in 1826 and served as deacon for forty years. Principally a cattle dealer, he acquired several hundred acres in Antrim, including a sixty-acre pasture on Patten Hill that was subsequently developed as White Birch Point. He also owned water rights along Great Brook. Tryphena died in 1818, and Amos married Hannah Heald in 1821. He erected a large brick house in 1827, and retired from active farming in 1848. He died, August 15, 1865, at age ninety-six.

Second

George Parmenter and wife Lucinda Green bought his father's farm in 1848 and there raised their four surviving offspring. George, less entrepreneurial than his father, made a living as a skilled mechanic and hired laborer in addition to farming his land. George sold some of the property acquired by Amos, including the Patten Hill pasture and water rights on Great Brook. As the seventh consecutive son born to Amos and Tryphena, George was believed to have the gift of healing and was credited with numerous cures for which he charged no fee. Lucinda fed and boarded patients who arrived for treatment, receiving payment for that service. George died in 1890 and Lucinda in 1900.

Third

Abbie Laurella, youngest daughter of George and Lucinda, married Bill Butterfield in 1866, and together they raised eight children. Abbie took after her grandfather, purchasing land in her own name before she and Bill bought the family farm from her widowed mother and other heirs in 1890. Bill (his formal name) operated an orchard and engaged in poultry farming. Two years after acquiring the Parmenter place, Abbie died by her own hand, her response to a diagnosis of cancer. Bill, a pensioned veteran of the Civil War, died in 1908.

Fourth

Charles Butterfield, second child of Bill and Abbie, married Annie Goodwin and joined his father in the poultry business after his mother died. He acquired property rights from his siblings and obtained a long-term lease from his widower father, and thus essentially owned the farm where he and Annie raised their seven children. During and after his full-time poultry farming, Charles was long engaged in school and town affairs. In addition to farming, he operated a general store until he died in 1933. Annie remained in the farmhouse from which she died in 1961.

Fifth

Byron, firstborn of Charles and Annie, married Vera McClure following his service in World War I. They moved to the farm after his father died, and through the extraordinary generosity of his siblings Byron acquired the heavily mortgaged farm from his mother. Byron and Vera raised their two children, Isabel and Charles, on the farm even as they labored together to make the farm a paying proposition. Mainly, their income was derived from dairy farming, Byron turning much of the land into pasture for their cattle. With supplemental income derived from Byron's considerable skill as carpenter, mason and lumberman, the farm emerged from debt intact. Vera died in 1970 and Byron in 1971.

Sixth

Isabel (Butterfield) Nichols and her brother Charles inherited the farm from their father Byron, but with no interest in farming, for thirty-five years rented out the large farmhouse and barn to family members while the farmland itself began the journey into wildness. The farmhouse and immediately surrounding acreage was purchased by their second cousin, Marie Harriman, great-great-great-great-granddaughter of Amos Parmenter, and she resides there with her husband Chris Condon.

Seventh

Isabel Nichol's three older children from her first marriage to Charles McLean II, Nancy, Charles and Jane, were given the remaining thirty-three acres of Butterfield Farm when their mother died in 2005. It is that portion of Butterfield Farm that is featured in this book. The land is currently on the market.

Eighth

William Nichols, son of Isabel and her second husband Martin Nichols, married Barbara Boule and the couple raised two sons, Stephen and Jonathan, in the house William built in one of his grandfather Byron Butterfield's pastures. Though now divorced, Barbara has remained on the land, and the couple's adult sons may very well someday acquire an interest in that piece of the original Parmenter place where they grew up.

Notes

Page 1   Epigram, Raymo, *The Path*, Walker Publishing Company, 2003, p. 3.

Page 6   "He had great difficulty . . .": Cochrane, *History of the Town of Antrim, New Hampshire,* 1880, pp. 636–637.

Page 7   "If you can learn . . .": Michaels, *Fugitive Pieces*, Vintage Books, 1998, p. 82.

Page 9   Epigram: Rilke, *Letters on Life: New Prose Translations,* Urich Baer, translator, Modern Library Classics, 2006, p. 7.

Page 12   "Terry Tempest Williams . . .": Repetation is described in *When Women Were Birds*, Sarah Chrichton Books, 2012, pp. 163–164.

Page 13   "Who we are now . . .": Rezendes, *The Wild Within*, Jeremy P. Tarcher/Putnam, 1999, p. 15.

Page 14   "The usefulness of hair . . .": Snyder, *Earth House Hold*, New Directions, 1969, p. 19.

Page 20   Solastalgia and soliphilia are discussed in *New York Times Magazine*, January 31, 2010, pp. 36–41.

Page 21   "The speculations, intuitions, and formal ideas . . .": Lopez, *Vintage Lopez*, Vintage Books, 2004, pp. 6–7.

Page 25   Epigram: "Mending Wall," *The Poems of Robert Frost*, Random House Modern Library, 1946, p. 35.

Page 29   "An illusion so desired . . .": *Collected Poems of Wallace Stevens*, Alfred A. Knopf, 1971, p. 525.

Page 32   Pillows and cradles are discussed in Wessels, *Reading the Forested Landscape*, The Countryman Press, 1997, pp 113–115.

Page 38   "To me, performing the 30 variations . . .": Liner notes, Musical Heritage Society.

Page 38   "It is hard to know rocks . . .": Henry David Thoreau, *The Journal of Henry D. Thoreau* (undated), Vol. I, p. 469, Dover Publications, 1962.

CHARLES BUTTERFIELD

Page 39 "April 13, Began our spring work today...": Typescript of Dennison Gould's diary, James A. Tuttle Library, Antrim, NH.

Page 41 "plow terrace": Wessels, *Forest Forensics*, Countryman Press, 2010, pp. 99–102.

Page 44 "As the earth warmed...": Kolbert, *Field Notes from a Catastrophe*, Bloomsbury, 2006, p. 85.

Page 45 "Mr Parmenter Sir Please...": Order slip, part of author's private collection.

Page 51 "The Wood-Pile": *The Poems of Robert Frost*, Random House Modern Library, 1946, p. 112.

Page 53 Tom Wessels, *Forest Forensics*, Countryman Press, 2010.

Page 56 "On this occasion...": Cochrane, *History of the Town of Antrim*, p. 460.

Page 59 "thence northerly on said Gregg's...": Amos Parmenter's deed to George Parmenter in author's private collection.

Page 63 Epigram: Thoreau, *The Journal of Henry D. Thoreau*, July 6, 1852, Vol. IV, p. 193, Dover Publications, 1962.

Page 67 Alld's real estate transactions recorded in Tibbals, *Genealogical Record, Antrim, NH, Families,* 1967, p. 17. Also, miscellaneous records, Antrim Historical Society.

Page 68 "That the territory...": Whiton, *History of the Town of Antrim, New Hampshire, 1744–1844*, p. 14.

Page 69 "It is through the power of observation...": Lopez, *Vintage Lopez*, p. 96.

Page 71 "Round every circle...": *Selections from Ralph Waldo Emerson*, Houghton-Mifflin Company, 1957, p. 168.

Page 73 "I look up the creek...": Dillard, *Pilgrim at Tinker Creek*, Harper and Row, 1985, p. 100.

Page 76 "Again I scent the white lily...": Thoreau, *The Journal of Henry D. Thoreau*, June 16, 1854, Vol. VI, p. 352, Dover Publications, 1962.

Page 79 "cattle caught in the mud...": Whiton, *History of the Town of Antrim*, p. 82.

Page 80 "Little Pond, half a mile south-west...": Whiton, p. 82.

Page 82 "Began to hook up the virgin mould...": Thoreau, *Walden*, Random House Modern Library College Editions, 1950, p. 263.

SEEKING PARMENTER

Page 84   "Most men, even in this comparatively free country . . .": *Walden*, pp. 5–6.

Page 84   "How near to good . . .": Thoreau, "Walking, " *The Essays of Henry D. Thoreau*, Lewis Hyde, ed., North Point Press, 2002, p. 163.

Page 86   "The field of water betrays . . .": Thoreau, *Walden*, p. 171.

Page 87   McKibben, *End of Nature*, Anchor Books, 1999.

Page 111   "You know, I think if people stay . . .": Snyder, *The Practice of the Wild*, North Point Press, 1990, p. 39.

Page 117   Epigram: Beston, *The Outermost House*, Henry Holt and Company (Owl Books), 1992, p. 218.

Page 119   Hebert, *The Old American*, University Press of New England, 2000.

Page 120   Chamovitz, *What a Plant Knows*, Scientific American/Farrar, Straus, Giroux, 2012.

Page 123   "How would the rest of nature respond . . .": Weisman, *The World Without Us*, Picador, 2007, p. 5.

Page 126   "Nature is everything . . .": Carruth, *Selected Essays & Reviews*, Copper Canyon Press, 1996, p. 353.

Page 128   "When you know one place well . . .": Raymo, *The Path*, p. 5.

Page 130   "Grandsir' met me at the depot . . .": Journal of Mary Evangeline Hartman (née Butterfield), part of the author's private collection.

Acknowledgments

I thank Charlene Ellis, William Edelglass, Charles McLean, Helen Neswald, Ryan Owens, Bob Parks, Chuck Ratte, Tom Wessels, Arthur Westing, and Dick Winslow for reading and commenting on the manuscript in whole or in part at various stages. I thank Muriel Wolf for reading the entire manuscript with great sensitivity and arranging a public reading. I thank Lyman Gilmore, editor of *The Limrik*, for publishing excerpts from the manuscript. I thank my grandnephew Chuck McLean for his delightful renderings based on my photographs of the Parmenter/Butterfield farm as it now stands. My wife Nancy assisted me in the genealogical research and by copyediting the typewritten pages repeatedly, and I thank her for all her help and support and, above all, her faith in me, and her love. I thank Sid Hall for believing in *Seeking Parmenter* enough to edit and publish it, and I thank Kirsty Walker for her guidance in marketing the finished product. I especially appreciated the free meals and good company Ben Pratt and Diane Chauncey provided when I was camping in Antrim.

CHARLES BUTTERFIELD

About the Author

CHARLES BUTTERFIELD, at age four, moved with his parents from downtown Antrim to the family farm in Clinton, and for twenty years he raised animals, milked cows, and worked in hayfields and in the woods. From farm life he went on to become an award-winning biology and chemistry teacher. Raised in a household filled with books and music, he came naturally to writing, singing and playing keyboard. Long retired from teaching, he continues to write poems, essays, short fiction and historical nonfiction, and occasionally plays organ and piano in area churches. Charles and his wife Nancy live on a large, second-growth farm in Hinsdale, New Hampshire, which they have protected through a conservation easement with Monadnock Conservancy.

About the Illustrator

CHUCK MCLEAN, the author's grandnephew, is the designer at Timberline Signs in Rye, New Hampshire. He lives in Rochester, New Hampshire, with wife Susan and their young sons Owen and Liam.